The Modern Cook

For Jenny, Alex and Grace

First published in 2001 by New Holland Publishers (NZ) Ltd
Auckland • Sydney • London • Cape Town

www.newhollandpublishers.com

218 Lake Road, Northcote, Auckland, New Zealand
14 Aquatic Drive, Frenchs Forest, NSW 2086, Australia
86 Edgware Road, London W2 2EA, United Kingdom
80 McKenzie Street, Cape Town 8001, South Africa

Copyright © 2001 in text: Ray McVinnie
Copyright © 2001 in photography: Kieran Scott
Copyright © 2001 New Holland Publishers (NZ) Ltd

ISBN: 1 877246 54 9

Managing editor: Renée Lang
Cover and text design: Gerrard Malcolm
Editors: Barbara Nielsen and Penny Bieder

10 9 8 7 6 5 4 3 2 1

Colour reproduction by Colourscan (Singapore)
Printed by Craft Print Pte Ltd Singapore

Ray McVinnie
The Modern Cook

Photographed by Kieran Scott

NEW HOLLAND

Contents

Introduction   6

Steamed Mussels: a succulent feast   8

Omelette: simple, cheap and honest   16

A Dressed Salad: refreshingly tart   26

Vegetable Stirfries: appetising crunchiness   36

Roast Chicken: meltingly tender   46

Panfried Steak: juicy tenderness   56

Panfried Fish: golden perfection   68

Vegetable Soup: restorative comfort food   78

Roasted Vegetables: perfumed with garlic   86

Stew: slowly, slowly, slowly   96

Steamed Rice and Risotto: essential grains   108

Dried Pasta: tender to the bite   120

Dried Noodles: asian cool   130

Pound Cake: smack your lips   140

Fruit: colour, fragrance, flavour   148

What a Cook Needs   156

Index   158

To become a modern cook all you need to be able to do is perfect some basic recipes, which then become a foundation for you to build on. A sort of 'mixing and matching' of ideas that you know will work. These ideas will almost certainly be based on recipes that you're comfortable with, recipes that can be added to as your confidence and creativity expand.

The Modern Cook essentially represents a selection of my own basic recipes that I've developed over the years. Its purpose is to turn you into someone who can confidently produce delicious, unpretentious food, using what you have available in the fridge or cupboard, what is cheap or what is in season. It's about the preparation, eating and sharing of healthy food, and seeing this as an important and enjoyable part of your life.

Take chicken for example – most people yearn to be able to turn out a crispy-skinned, golden, melt-in-the-mouth roast chicken. I'll show you how to get it right and, once you've mastered my basic recipe, you'll be able to branch out and turn that same roast chicken into a number of different meals. For example, that roast chicken can become a hot salad. Or you could stuff the chicken before roasting and then serve it on a baked potato gratin. Another chicken variation involves serving it with stirfried noodles – the list goes on!

This principle of mastering a basic recipe and then developing it further is applied to various cooking methods, including stirfrying, roasting, making omelettes, soups and stews, panfrying, steaming, cooking with rice, pasta and Asian noodles, and some stunning dessert ideas. Each one has up to six variations, adding up to nearly 100 recipes, which still leaves plenty of scope for you to expand on all and any of them in your own way.

It's worth noting that cooking shouldn't be just a matter of learning recipes off by heart and blindly following instructions. Every time you make something it's likely to be slightly different. Overall, food can be an infuriatingly unstable commodity so you need to pay attention at every stage, from buying to serving. And this is where your senses need to become attuned to the changes in food as it is prepared and cooked.

It can be a process of trial and error, but when a dish you've made is particularly successful the idea is to make a mental 'snapshot' of how it tastes, feels, sounds or smells so that you know what to aim for next time. Before long it will become second nature for you to be aware of certain things without

Introduction

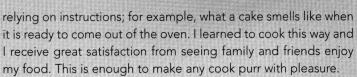

relying on instructions; for example, what a cake smells like when it is ready to come out of the oven. I learned to cook this way and I receive great satisfaction from seeing family and friends enjoy my food. This is enough to make any cook purr with pleasure.

Presentation is another important part of being a modern cook – you don't have to present your food as if you were a restaurant chef. Leave that to the professionals. Instead, invest in some large white platters so that people can help themselves – the visual impact of an artfully heaped platter can be stunning. It should all look natural, as if it got onto the platter by itself – keep the garnish simple, make sure it's related to the dish and that you can eat it.

So go for it – make the basic recipes in this book part of your repertoire and build on them to create your own style.

RAY MCVINNIE

A succulent feast

Steamed Mussels

Fresh, steaming hot mussels, the friendly seafood,
provide a wonderful instant feast, and are as great
as an accompaniment to other fish as they are on
their own.

Mussels with Leeks and Bacon
Mussels in Chilli Broth with Noodles
Mussels with Herbed Rice and
    Lemon Mayonnaise
Panfried Fish with Mussels and Cream
Stirfried Chinese Greens with Mussels

Basic Recipe

Steamed Mussels with White Wine

The French certainly know how to cook mussels. This is my version of the retro classic, Moules Marinières, a simple yet flavoursome handling of mussels. Whenever I cook this I am always astounded at just how good such a simple combination of flavours can taste. Even though the inspiration for this dish is old-fashioned, the robust, satisfying flavour and simplicity of the dish make it a perfect component for any modern cook's repertoire.

24 medium-sized (about 80mm/3in long) mussels	200ml (7fl oz) dry white wine	2 tablespoons unsalted butter
2 cloves garlic	2 tablespoons chopped flat-leafed parsley	freshly ground black pepper

Clean the mussels as described in The Rules below. Peel and finely chop the garlic.

Put all ingredients except the butter and pepper into a large, wide saucepan and bring to the boil. Boil until the mussels open, removing each of them to a warm serving bowl as they open, remembering that they are ready when the flesh of the mussel has come away from the shell.

When all the mussels have been removed, stir in the butter and season with pepper. Pour the sauce over the mussels and serve with plenty of crusty bread to mop up the sauce.

This very simple dish is just as good served with steaming hot Italian spaghetti, cooked al dente, or hot steamed long grain rice.

SERVES 4

The Rules

The fact that mussels are often the cheapest seafood is one of their major attributes. For a relatively small cost you can buy a first-class fresh ingredient that can be transformed into a succulent feast to feed a crowd. It is well worth knowing how to cook mussels.

Always buy live mussels. You will know they are alive because the shells will close when given a sharp tap. Discard any cracked or broken mussels. Wash them well, scrub the shells, chipping off any barnacles or limpets, and pull out the beard – the seaweed-like filaments which hang out of the shell when it is closed. Pull the beard towards the rounded end of the shell and pull it out.

When cooking mussels pay attention. Overcooked mussels are tough and unpleasant and, as they will not all open at the same time, you need to stand over the pan and remove them as they open and you notice that the flesh of the mussel has come away from the shell.

Remember also that the liquor that comes out of the mussel is very salty, so refrain from seasoning with salt until you have tasted the dish.

Make sure you have the right saucepan to cook mussels in. It needs to be big enough to fit them all comfortably. I use my wide, deep stainless steel risotto pan, which provides a large area of heat to come in contact with the mussels. It means they will all still continue cooking if I leave the lid off once they start to open and I want to begin removing them. It also means that they are not packed deeply, which would make it hard to pull out the ones that cook first at the bottom.

Mussels with Leeks and Bacon

This dish is based on the same sort of sofrito used in the Stew chapter. ('Sofrito' is a Spanish term for the initial frying. The technique is explained fully in The Rules on page 99.) Like all sofritos it forms the flavour-base of the dish and should be cooked slowly.

24 medium-sized mussels
4 leeks
4 tablespoons olive oil
3 cloves garlic, finely chopped

1 large sprig fresh thyme
3 rashers rindless bacon, chopped
2 tablespoons chopped
 flat-leafed parsley

200ml (7fl oz) dry white wine
extra parsley for garnish

Clean the mussels as described in The Rules opposite. Peel the outer leaves off the leeks, trim the ends, thinly slice the leeks, and wash and drain them well.

Heat the olive oil over a moderate heat and add the garlic, thyme, bacon, leeks and parsley. Fry gently, without browning, until the leeks are soft and look transparent.

Add the wine and mussels and bring to the boil. Cover until the mussels start to open and cook as described in the Basic Recipe opposite. Uncover the pan and remove each mussel as it opens and place on a warm serving dish.

Pour the leek mixture over the mussels, mix, and sprinkle with chopped parsley. Serve with plenty of bread. **SERVES 4**

See also: The Rules for stew, page 99.

Mussels in Chilli Broth with Noodles

Asian comfort food, this dish is great for cold nights when you want something that tastes delicious and is good for you. As a change, try a few chunks of skinned, boned fish thrown in as the mussels cook.

24 medium-sized mussels
1 spring onion
300g (10½ oz) thick Chinese
 egg noodles

2 tablespoons peanut oil
1 stick lemongrass
2 small fresh red chillies
2 slices peeled ginger

1 litre (1 pint 15fl oz) well-flavoured
 liquid chicken or fish stock
1 tablespoon thinly sliced
 coriander root and stalk

Clean the mussels as described in The Rules opposite. Thinly slice the spring onion on the diagonal.

Cook the noodles as described in the Basic Recipe on page 132. Drain them well and toss with the peanut oil to stop them sticking together. Divide the noodles evenly among four large, deep soup bowls.

Discard the coarse outer leaves of the lemongrass and use the bulbous end only, squashed with the side of a knife. Remove the

seeds from the chillies and thinly slice the chillies. Put the ginger, stock, lemongrass, chillies and coriander into a large saucepan and bring to the boil. Simmer for 2 minutes then add the mussels and cook until the mussels open. Put six mussels into each bowl.

Bring the broth back to the boil, discard the ginger and lemongrass and pour the broth over the mussels and noodles in the bowls. Sprinkle the spring onion on top.

SERVES 4

See also: the Basic Recipe for noodles, page 132.

Mussels with Herbed Rice and Lemon Mayonnaise

The pungent, sweet iodine taste of mussels goes well with savoury herbed rice and the sharp richness of homemade lemon mayonnaise.

LEMON MAYONNAISE
2 egg yolks
1 clove garlic, crushed to a paste
finely grated zest of 1 large lemon
200ml (7fl oz) extra virgin olive oil
juice of 1 large lemon
salt

HERBED RICE
4 shallots
3 tablespoons olive oil
3 cloves garlic, finely chopped
1 tablespoon fresh thyme leaves
1 thumb-length sprig of rosemary
1 teaspoon salt
400g (14oz) long grain white rice
125ml (4fl oz) dry white wine
500ml (18fl oz) water
1 tablespoon butter
2 tablespoons chopped
    flat-leafed parsley
10 basil leaves, ripped into
    small pieces

MUSSELS
24 medium-sized mussels
4 tablespoons olive oil
1 clove garlic, finely chopped

See also: The Rules for mussels, page 10.

Whisk the egg yolks, garlic and lemon zest in a food processor or in a bowl with a whisk, until well mixed. Start adding the extra virgin olive oil, drop by drop, stirring continuously.

When you see the mixture start to thicken and look creamy (not grainy and thin), start adding the oil in a very thin trickle. Stir continuously until all the oil is used and the mixture is thick and buttery. Stir in the lemon juice. Season with salt to taste and set aside.

If the mixture refuses to thicken and is grainy and thin, it means you have added the oil too quickly. You can fix it by pouring the curdled mixture into a bowl and setting it aside. Completely clean the processor bowl or the bowl you were working in. Get a fresh egg yolk and the remaining oil (or more oil) and start again, this time adding the oil very slowly. Once you see the mixture thicken as it should, then start adding the curdled mixture slowly, stirring continuously until it is all incorporated.

Peel and finely chop the shallots. Heat the olive oil for the rice in a saucepan over a moderate heat. Add the shallots, garlic, thyme, rosemary and salt. Fry gently without browning, until the shallots are soft.

Wash and drain the rice well. Add it to the pan, mix well, then add the wine and bring to the boil. Boil until all of the wine has evaporated, stirring occasionally.

Add the water, bring to the boil, cover tightly, and turn the heat down to the lowest setting and cook for 20 minutes without uncovering for any reason. Remove from the heat and let it stand, covered, for 5 minutes.

Uncover, add the butter, parsley and basil and fluff up the rice with a fork, mixing in the herbs gently.

Clean the mussels as described in The Rules on page 10. Put the olive oil, the garlic and mussels into a saucepan. Cover and place over a high heat. Keep the pan covered and shake it. Uncover now and again to see when the mussels start to open. Do not worry, they will not burn because the mussels will release enough liquor to steam them open. Remove the mussels from the pan as they open.

Serve the mussels and any of their liquor on the rice with a dollop of the lemon mayonnaise on the top.

SERVES 4

Mussels with Herbed Rice and Lemon Mayonnaise

Panfried Fish with Mussels and Cream

20 medium-sized mussels
50ml (2fl oz) dry white wine
4 x 150g (5oz) firm white skinless,
    boneless fish fillets

plain flour for dusting
4 tablespoons olive oil
grated zest of 1 lemon
125ml (4fl oz) cream

2 tablespoons chopped chives
freshly ground black pepper

See also: The Rules and the Basic Recipe for mussels, page 10; the Basic Recipe for fish, page 70; and the Basic Recipe for salad, page 29.

Clean the mussels as described in The Rules on page 10. Put the mussels and wine into a wide saucepan and cook as described in the Basic Recipe on page 10. Cool the mussels and remove them from the shells. Strain and reserve the liquor from the mussels.

Preheat the oven to 200°C (400°F). Dust the fish in flour and shake off the excess. Heat the olive oil over a moderate heat and add the fish. Panfry on each side until golden brown then transfer from the pan onto an ovenproof dish and place in the oven to finish cooking as described in the Basic Recipe on page 70, while you make the sauce.

Pour the oil from the pan and wipe it out with paper towels. Add the mussel liquor, the lemon zest and cream and bring to the boil. Boil rapidly until the mixture has slightly thickened, add the chives, taste and season with pepper.

Add the mussels, bring the sauce back to the boil but do not boil the mussels for too long as they will toughen.

Remove the fish from the oven, pour any juices from the fish into the sauce and mix. Pour the sauce over the fish. Serve with crusty bread and follow with a green salad – see the Basic Recipe on page 29.

SERVES 4

Stirfried Chinese Greens with Mussels

The mussels and greens are cooked in a very hot wok and are kept constantly moving. The mussels will have opened by the time the greens are tender but still crisp.
Chinese greens are available from some supermarkets and most Asian shops. Spinach, cabbage and broccoli can be used if Chinese greens are unavailable.

See also: The Rules for mussels, page 10.

24 medium-sized mussels
5 cloves garlic
3 tablespoons peanut oil

2 tablespoons finely chopped
    fresh ginger
2 dried red chillies
4 spring onions

4 baby bok choy
1 bunch gai lan
2 tablespoons oyster sauce

Clean the mussels as described in The Rules on page 10. Peel and finely chop the garlic. Heat a wok until very hot, add the peanut oil and swirl it around the wok. Add the garlic, ginger and chillies and stirfry for 15–20 seconds. Add the mussels, the spring onions sliced on the diagonal, the bok choy sliced into quarters lengthways, the gai lan with thick stalks sliced thinly on the diagonal and the oyster sauce. Stirfry over a high heat until the mussels have opened and the greens are tender but still crisp.

Serve immediately on boiled thick egg noodles or steamed long grain white rice.

SERVES 4

Omelette

Omelettes may seem a homely choice in a cookbook that purports to be modern, but there are many delicious and often forgotten ways of cooking lightly beaten eggs in a frying pan.

Tortilla de Patatas
Chilli Omelette with Spiced Potatoes
Spicy Pork Omelette with Fried Rice
Roasted Pumpkin and Feta Frittata
Prawn Omelette with Cold Rice Noodle Salad

Simple, cheap and honest

Basic Recipe

Fresh Herb Omelette

This is a recipe for one person. It is better to make several omelettes in quick succession than it is to double or triple the mix, as they are quick to make. Too much mixture will not cook properly and is too unwieldy to manage.

2 tablespoons butter or olive oil
2 eggs, lightly beaten with a fork

1 teaspoon each of chopped
chives, chervil and tarragon

salt and freshly ground
black pepper

Heat a 25cm (10in) frying pan over moderate heat. Add the butter or olive oil and turn the heat up a little. When the butter bubbles and is about to change colour, or the oil is hot but not smoking, add the eggs and swirl them around the pan by tilting it in a circular motion.

Put the pan back on the heat and keep pulling the edges of the mixture away from the sides of the pan so that the uncooked mixture flows into the empty parts of the pan. Quickly sprinkle the herbs over the omelette, season it well with salt and pepper, fold in half and slide it onto a hot plate. The outside will be browned and the inside, although slightly runny to begin with, will soon cook with the heat of the omelette. Serve immediately. **SERVES 1**

The Rules

When making an omelette, use the freshest eggs possible and do not over-beat them. They should be beaten enough so that you can't see the difference between the white and the yolk, but the eggs should still be viscous and not completely runny. If you lift some of the egg up with the fork, it should still feel gelatinous.

Olive oil or butter can be used to fry eggs and is a matter of taste. I prefer the taste and health advantages of olive oil.

There is no nutritional difference between white and brown eggs – the breed and diet of the hen that laid the egg determines its colour and flavour. Free-range or organic eggs generally have a better yolk colour and flavour than commercially raised eggs.

When choosing eggs be sure that the shell is intact; if it is cracked, its contents may have been contaminated.

Fresh eggs, refrigerated immediately, will keep for about 2 weeks. (Check the use-by date when buying.) Keep them, pointed end down, in the carton you bought them in rather than in egg racks – the shells are porous and will absorb strong flavours if exposed to them in the fridge. Remove eggs from the refrigerator 30 minutes before using them to let them come up to room temperature.

Egg whites will keep for up to 2 days in the refrigerator and can be frozen. Thaw them when needed, use the same day and do not refreeze. Egg yolks should be kept in the refrigerator, covered with cold water, and will keep for only 1–2 days.

If you are lucky enough to have hens, you will know your eggs are freshly laid, but most purchased eggs take a while to reach you.

Test an egg for freshness by putting it into a large bowl of cold water. If it sinks and lies on its side it is fresh. This is because the air pocket inside the egg has not yet shrunk with age. If the egg floats near the middle of the water, rounded end up, it could be several weeks old, which does not mean it is stale. But if it floats near the top of the water, rounded end up, it is too old to use. If in doubt, break it into a small bowl before using to check, or judge by the use-by date on the carton.

A fresh egg is one that has a plump, thick white that clings to the yolk, holding it in place after it is broken onto a plate. Thin, watery whites are a sign that an egg is not fresh.

Tortilla de Patatas

Tortilla de Patatas, or Espanola, is the thick, hearty potato omelette/cake that is served all over Spain. Sometimes it will be served hot on the breakfast table, but it is more likely to be served cold in small wedges or squares to enjoy as tapas with drinks. Tortilla de Patatas is a deliciously robust dish that illustrates the best characteristics of Spanish food and is always a crowd pleaser.

2 cloves garlic
2 onions
900g (2lb) waxy potatoes

3 tablespoons olive oil
salt and freshly ground
black pepper

8 eggs, lightly beaten
4 tablespoons olive oil for frying

Peel and finely chop the garlic. Peel and thinly slice the onions and potatoes.

Heat the 3 tablespoons of olive oil over a moderate heat in a 25cm (10in) diameter heavy frying pan. Add the garlic, onions and potatoes, turn the heat to low and fry, covered, for about 25 minutes, without browning, until the potatoes are tender. Season well with salt and pepper to taste.

Remove the potato mixture from the pan, let it cool slightly then add it to the eggs.

In a clean pan, heat the 4 tablespoons of olive oil over a moderate heat and add the mixture. Gently cook over a low heat, shaking occasionally, until the bottom is set. Cover the top with a large dinner plate, invert the pan so that the tortilla sits on the plate, uncooked side down, then slide the tortilla back into the pan to cook the other side.

When the tortilla is completely set, remove from the pan and serve, preferably cold, in wedges or squares. SERVES 6–8

Chilli Omelette with Spiced Potatoes

Here an omelette is used as a wrapping for the spiced potatoes and makes a good vegetarian meal. Kalonji are the black seeds of the nigella plant, available from Asian shops.

See also: the Basic Recipe for omelette, page 18.

800g (1lb 12oz) waxy potatoes
1 dried red chilli
4 cloves garlic
1 onion
4 tablespoons peanut oil
1½ tablespoons finely chopped
fresh ginger

1 teaspoon ground turmeric
½ teaspoon kalonji
1 teaspoon fennel seeds
1 tablespoon ground cumin
grated zest of 1 lemon
1 teaspoon salt
400ml (14fl oz) water

juice of ½ lemon
8 eggs
4 dried red chillies, finely chopped
coriander leaves

Boil the potatoes in their skins until just tender, peel then break into large pieces. Seed the chilli and chop finely. Peel and finely chop the garlic. Peel and chop the onion.

Heat the peanut oil in a large, deep frying pan over a moderate heat. Add the onion, ginger and garlic and fry gently, without browning, until the onion is soft.

Add the chilli, turmeric, kalonji, fennel seeds, cumin and lemon zest. Mix well and fry gently, without browning, for 1 minute. Add the salt and potatoes and mix well.

Add the water and bring to the boil. Simmer until most of the water has evaporated and the mixture is thick, about 15 minutes. Add the lemon juice and mix well. Keep warm.

Break 2 eggs into each of four bowls, add a chopped dried red chilli to each and lightly beat.

Make four omelettes, one after another, as described in the Basic Recipe on page 18, but omit the herbs. Before folding each omelette in half, put some of the spiced potatoes on one side of the omelette, then fold it and slide it onto a plate. Sprinkle each omelette with coriander leaves.

SERVES 4

Spicy Pork Omelette with Fried Rice

SPICY PORK OMELETTE
200g (7oz) skinned, boned loin of pork
3 cloves garlic
4 tablespoons peanut oil
2 small dried red chillies, thinly sliced
1 tablespoon finely chopped fresh ginger
5 eggs, lightly beaten
2 tablespoons soy sauce

FRIED RICE
3 cloves garlic
1 onion
1 small carrot
4 tablespoons peanut oil
2 tablespoons finely chopped fresh ginger
1 stick celery, thinly sliced
500g (1lb 2oz) leftover steamed long grain white rice
3 tablespoons oyster sauce

75g (3oz) unsalted roasted peanuts, coarsely chopped
2 tablespoons finely sliced coriander stalks
3 spring onions, finely sliced
4–5 leaves iceberg lettuce, thinly sliced

Cut the pork into 1cm (1/2 in) cubes. Peel and finely chop the garlic.

Heat 2 tablespoons of the peanut oil for the pork omelette in a 25cm (10in) frying pan until hot and add the pork, chillies, ginger and garlic. Fry gently, stirring occasionally, until the pork is well cooked and browned. Transfer the mixture from the pan to a bowl.

Clean the pan and place it over a moderate heat. Add the remaining 2 tablespoons of peanut oil and let it get hot. Add the eggs and swirl them around the pan by tilting it in a circular motion. Put the pan back on the heat and keep pulling the edges of the mixture away from the sides of the pan so that the uncooked mixture flows into the empty parts of the pan. Sprinkle the pork mixture and soy sauce over the top and fold the omelette in half. Transfer to a large plate, cool and slice thinly. Set aside.

Peel and finely chop the garlic and onion. Peel and finely dice the carrot. Heat a wok until hot and add the peanut oil for the rice, then the garlic, ginger, onion, carrot and celery. Stirfry until the onion is transparent but still crisp. Add the rice and oyster sauce and mix well. Stirfry until the rice is hot. Add the peanuts, coriander, spring onions and lettuce and mix well.

Put the rice onto a warm serving platter and sprinkle the sliced omelette on top. Serve with soy and chilli sauces in small bowls on the side.

SERVES 4

Roasted Pumpkin and Feta Frittata

This is an omelette made in a frying pan but finished in the oven. Made at home with good ingredients and carefully cooked, it in no way resembles the lifeless slabs of so-called frittata one can sometimes see in second-rate cafés. Roasting the pumpkin intensifies the sweet flavour, which goes well with the salty feta and the creamy eggs. Frittata is excellent for a light lunch, or cold as picnic food.

ROASTED PUMPKIN
500g (1lb 2oz) peeled, seeded
  pumpkin
3 tablespoons olive oil
salt and freshly ground
  black pepper

FRITTATA
2 tablespoons pumpkin seeds
1 large onion
3 cloves garlic
6 tablespoons olive oil
2 tablespoons chopped
  coriander stalks

reserved pumpkin
200g (7oz) feta
6 eggs, lightly beaten

Preheat the oven to 200°C (400°F). Cut the pumpkin into 3cm chunks and put it into a roasting dish, add the olive oil, mix well and season with salt and pepper. Roast until well cooked and browned, about 30–40 minutes. Remove from the oven and reserve. Leave the oven on.

Toast the pumpkin seeds over a moderate heat in a dry pan until all have 'popped'. Peel and chop the onion. Peel and finely chop the garlic.

Heat 3 tablespoons of the olive oil over a moderate heat and add the onion, garlic and coriander. Fry gently, without browning, until the onion is soft.

Add the onion mix to the reserved roasted pumpkin and add the feta, crumbled into small, bite-sized lumps. Carefully mix.

Clean the pan, put it back over a moderate heat and add the remaining 3 tablespoons of olive oil. When the oil is hot add the eggs and cook for 30 seconds.

Sprinkle the pumpkin mixture evenly over the surface of the eggs, shake the pan and put it into the oven. Cook the frittata until completely set, about 25 minutes.

Remove from the oven, run a knife around the inside edge of the pan and slide a spatula under the frittata. Invert the pan onto a large plate to remove the frittata. Serve cut into wedges with spicy chutney and salad.

SERVES 4–6

Roasted Pumpkin and Feta Frittata

Prawn Omelette with Cold Rice Noodle Salad

A light South-east Asian-inspired dish where the omelette becomes a deluxe ingredient in the salad. Pay attention to balancing the sweet, salty, sour and hot tastes. Rice noodles are available from Asian shops.

See also: the Basic Recipe for omelette, page 18.

PRAWN OMELETTE
3 tablespoons peanut oil
5 eggs, lightly beaten
250g (9oz) raw prawns, shelled
1 tablespoon chopped coriander
salt

DRESSING
3 tablespoons fish sauce
3 tablespoons sugar
1 tablespoon light soy sauce
1 tablespoon peanut oil
4 tablespoons rice vinegar

RICE NOODLE SALAD
3 cloves garlic
300g (10 1/2 oz) flat, wide
  rice noodles
1/2 cucumber
1 carrot
200g (7oz) fresh pineapple
2 tablespoons each chopped dill,
  mint and coriander
3 spring onions, thinly sliced
grated zest of 1 lemon
2 red chillies, thinly sliced
75g (3oz) roasted, shelled unsalted
  peanuts, crushed

Heat the peanut oil over a moderate heat in a 25cm (10in) frying pan. When it is hot add the eggs, swirl them around the pan and cook as described in the Basic Recipe on page 18.

Chop the prawns, drop into boiling water for 20 seconds and drain. Sprinkle the prawns and coriander over the top of the eggs and season with salt.

Finish cooking the omelette and fold it in half. Slide it onto a plate and let it cool. Slice it thinly and reserve.

Mix all the dressing ingredients together well until the sugar dissolves. Set aside.

Peel and finely chop the garlic. Soak the rice noodles in hot water until soft. Drop the soaked noodles into plenty of boiling water. When the water comes back to the boil, drain them well, cool them under cold water, drain well again and put into a large bowl.

Peel the cucumber, seed, and cut into 1cm (1/2 in) cubes. Peel the carrot and shave it down to nothing with a potato peeler. Peel and core the pineapple and cut into 2cm (3/4 in) cubes. Add the cucumber, carrot, pineapple, herbs, garlic, spring onions, lemon zest, chillies and dressing to the noodles.

Toss gently but well and sprinkle with the crushed peanuts. Serve in bowls with the reserved sliced prawn omelette on top.

SERVES 4

A Dressed

Salad

The range of salad leaves available to most of us can be quite bewildering. Experiment with different leaves and dressings, but treat them with care, as many are delicate.

Mussel, Spinach and Potato Salad
Roasted Red Onion and Beef Salad
Roast Chicken and Avocado Salad
   with Mustard Vinaigrette
Panfried Fish with Parsley and
   Caper Salad
Hot Spaghetti with Tomatoes, Rocket,
   Parmesan and Balsamic Vinegar
Panfried Steak on Olive, Rocket,
   Tomato and Bread Salad with
   Basil Vinaigrette

Green Salad with Vinaigrette

A green salad can be a mixture of leaves or just one type of leaf. Once you can make a perfect green salad you can use it as the basis of many other salads. Other vegetables can be added to it, for example, sliced avocados, roasted red capsicums (peppers), sundried tomatoes, cucumber, cherry tomatoes, thin carrot ribbons. Use it as a base for hot salads with panfried garlic prawns, panfried sliced chicken breast, panfried chicken livers, flaked smoked fish, smoked salmon, the list goes on.

Keep vinaigrette simple. How many 'special' recipe vinaigrettes have we all had to endure? Dressings for specific salads can, however, range from a simple olive oil and vinegar mixture to recipes using flavoured oils, yoghurt, lemon or lime juice, mustard, honey or herbs. Once you are used to making vinaigrette taste the way you like it, you may prefer simply to pour the oil and vinegar directly onto the salad, season it and toss it. Don't be afraid of vinaigrette, it is a sauce and there should be enough to give a light coating to each salad leaf without drowning the salad in grease.

1 clove garlic
50ml (2fl oz) extra virgin olive oil

1 tablespoon wine vinegar
enough salad greens for
    four people

salt and freshly ground
    black pepper

Peel and crush the garlic. Mix the extra virgin olive oil, wine vinegar and garlic together well. Season with salt and pepper to taste.

Just before serving, discard the garlic, pour the vinaigrette over the salad and toss with tongs or clean hands. Serve immediately.   **SERVES 4**

Basic Recipe

The Rules

'Salad' has become an all-encompassing term. As a light first course in the American manner, a salad is usually made of leaves with some other chopped or sliced ingredients such as tomatoes, cucumber or onions. After the main course in the French manner, a salad is made only of leaves and is a crunchy, juicy, tart palate-refresher before the cheese. Salads that include more substantial or hot, cooked ingredients are dishes that can stand alone, and are used as first courses or as a whole meal. The thing that unifies these seemingly diverse dishes is that they all have a dressing and can therefore be called salads.

Vegetables such as broccoli, cauliflower, green beans and fresh artichokes can be blanched in boiling water until they soften slightly, then dressed and eaten as a salad. Vegetables such as carrots, parsnips, courgettes (zucchini), eggplants (aubergines) and asparagus are good grilled or barbecued with a little olive oil, pepper and salt, then dressed and served as a salad.

The main points to remember when making a salad are:

- make sure all produce is in prime condition
- salad greens for four people will weigh about 125g (4½oz), otherwise a handful per person is about right
- if you are using mesclun salad, it is ready to use; if you are using mature lettuce leaves, these need to be ripped into manageable pieces but not too small
- use the best oil and vinegar you can afford; they do make a difference to a dressing
- make sure the dressing is well seasoned and do not mistake a lack of flavour for the need for more vinegar; the dressing may just need salt and pepper to bring out the flavour of the oil and vinegar
- if making up your own recipe for a salad, keep it simple; do not have too many tastes in one salad
- choose a large bowl when tossing a salad so that there is plenty of room to manoeuvre
- salads made with firm vegetables such as potatoes can be dressed ahead of time, but it is essential to dress leafy salads at the last minute or they will wilt and become slimy.

Mussel, Spinach and Potato Salad

Creamy, warm potatoes and mussels are perfect with the crunch of spinach and red onions.

CHILLI VINAIGRETTE
1 clove garlic
100ml (3 1/2 fl oz) extra virgin
    olive oil
2 tablespoons lemon juice
grated zest of 1 lemon
1 small fresh green chilli,
    finely chopped

See also: The Rules and the Basic Recipe for mussels, page 10.

1 teaspoon castor sugar
1 tablespoon chopped coriander
salt and freshly ground
    black pepper

SALAD
5 medium-sized waxy potatoes
1 small red onion

24 mussels
50ml (2fl oz) dry white wine
100g (3 1/2 oz) baby spinach leaves
1/2 red capsicum (pepper), cored,
    seeded and finely diced
2 gherkins, finely diced

Peel and finely chop the garlic. Mix all the vinaigrette ingredients together well, and season with salt and pepper to taste.

Peel the potatoes, cut them into bite-sized chunks, cook until tender in plenty of boiling salted water, drain well and cool slightly. Peel and finely chop the red onion. Clean the mussels as described in The Rules on page 10.

Put the mussels and wine into a large saucepan and bring to the boil. Cook as described in the Basic Recipe on page 10 and remove from the pan. As soon as they are cool enough to handle, shell the mussels.

Put the spinach, warm potatoes, onion, capsicum and gherkins into a large, wide salad bowl and add the mussels. Pour the vinaigrette over the salad, toss gently and serve. Good with steamed rice, spaghetti or crusty sourdough bread.   **SERVES 4–6**

Roasted Red Onion and Beef Salad

The rump steak weight is the trimmed weight, after all the fat and sinew has been removed.

4 medium-sized red onions
6 tablespoons olive oil
3 tablespoons wine vinegar
2 cloves garlic

1/2 teaspoon smoked sweet
    Spanish paprika
600g (1lb 5oz) rump steak
    in one piece
2 tablespoons capers

4 handfuls (125g/4 1/2 oz)
    mesclun salad
50ml (2fl oz) extra virgin olive oil
salt and freshly ground
    black pepper

Preheat the oven to 190°C (375°F). Leave the skin on the onions, but quarter them. Toss the onion quarters in 4 tablespoons of the olive oil and 2 tablespoons of the wine vinegar. Put the onions, olive oil and vinegar into a small roasting tray and roast for 20–25 minutes or until the onions are tender. Remove from the oven and set aside.

Peel the garlic and crush to a paste. Rub the garlic and paprika all over the steak and panfry it over a high heat in the remaining 2 tablespoons of olive oil until browned all over. Place the steak in the oven for 15 minutes to finish cooking until

medium rare. Remove from the oven and let it rest in a warm place for 10 minutes.

Put the onion quarters, the capers and the mesclun salad into a wide salad bowl or deep platter.

Mix the extra virgin olive oil with the remaining tablespoon of wine vinegar and season to taste with salt and pepper.

Pour this vinaigrette over the mesclun salad and quickly toss. Slice the steak thinly and pile on top of the salad. Serve immediately with crusty bread.   **SERVES 4–6**

Mussel, Spinach and Potato Salad

Roast Chicken and Avocado Salad with Mustard Vinaigrette

When I worked as a restaurant chef, a chicken and avocado salad was an essential feature of the lunchtime menu, especially for the 'ladies who lunch'. Many times one could hear a bejewelled matron confiding to the waiter, 'Oh no dear, I'm not eating, I'll just have the chicken salad'. The point about chicken salads is that everyone likes them, not just because they are deliciously inoffensive but also because they genuinely please.

MUSTARD VINAIGRETTE
1 small clove garlic
100ml (3^{1}/$_{2}$ fl oz) extra virgin
   olive oil
2 tablespoons wine vinegar
2 tablespoons wholegrain mustard
salt and freshly ground
   black pepper

CHICKEN AND AVOCADO SALAD
1 Basic Recipe Roast Chicken with
   Lemon and Garlic
2 ripe, firm Hass avocados
4 vine-ripened tomatoes
1 small red onion

1 Cos lettuce, leaves detached
   from the stem
8 black olives
8 basil leaves ripped into pieces
1 small handful coriander leaves

See also: *the Basic Recipe for chicken, page 48.*

Peel and finely chop the garlic. Mix all the vinaigrette ingredients together well, and season with salt and pepper to taste.

Roast the chicken as described in the Basic Recipe on page 48, but omit the gravy. Keep the chicken warm if you prefer a warm salad, otherwise cool it to room temperature. Carve the chicken, jointing the legs and wings and slicing the breast.

Halve, stone and peel the avocados and cut them into 1cm (^{1}/$_{2}$ in) thick slices. Core the tomatoes and cut into wedges. Peel and thinly slice the onion. Put the lettuce leaves into a wide, shallow salad bowl or platter.

Put the chicken, avocado, tomatoes, onion, olives, basil and coriander on top of the lettuce and pour the vinaigrette evenly over everything. Serve with crusty bread.

SERVES 6

Roast Chicken and Avocado Salad with Mustard Vinaigrette

Panfried Fish with Parsley and Caper Salad

The intensity of this chopped salad makes it more like a relish that goes with the fish.

**PARSLEY AND
CAPER SALAD**
2 lemons
1/2 cucumber
2 large handfuls flat-leafed
    parsley, chopped

1 handful rocket leaves, chopped
10 stoned black olives, finely sliced
2 tablespoons capers
50 ml (2fl oz) extra virgin olive oil
salt and freshly ground
    black pepper

PANFRIED FISH
4 x 200g (7oz) pieces firm white
    skinless, boneless fish

See also: the
Basic Recipe for
fish, page 70.

Peel the lemons with a sharp knife, slice the flesh away in wedge shapes from in between the pithy divisions and discard the pips, so that you have pithless, pipless lemon segments.

Peel the cucumber, split it in half lengthways, remove the seeds with a teaspoon and cut the flesh into 1cm (1/2 in) cubes.

Mix all the salad ingredients together and season with salt and pepper to taste. Set aside.

Panfry the fish pieces as described in the Basic Recipe on page 70, but omit the caper and lemon stage.

Serve the salad on top of the fried fish with baked floury potatoes or crusty bread.

SERVES 4

Hot Spaghetti with Tomatoes, Rocket, Parmesan and Balsamic Vinegar

Pasta salads can be loathsome things, but hot pasta with olive oil and vinegar can be delicious, as this dish is!

400g (14oz) Italian dried spaghetti
6 vine-ripened tomatoes
1 clove garlic
1 large handful rocket leaves

50ml (2fl oz) extra virgin olive oil
4 tablespoons balsamic vinegar
150g (5oz) parmesan cheese,
    shaved thinly

salt and freshly ground
    black pepper

See also: the
Basic Recipe for
pasta, page 122.

Cook the pasta as described in the Basic Recipe on page 122. Time this operation so that the pasta is drained, hot and ready for the other ingredients.

Core the tomatoes and cut them into thin wedges. Peel and finely chop the garlic.

Put the hot pasta into a warm bowl and add the remaining ingredients, season with salt and pepper to taste and give it all a careful toss. Serve immediately on hot plates. The rocket will wilt.

SERVES 4

Panfried Steak on Olive, Rocket, Tomato and Bread Salad with Basil Vinaigrette

A colourful salad that looks great piled, but untossed, on a shallow platter. It will become mixed as people help themselves. Using toasted, or in this case roasted, stale bread in salads is a Mediterranean tradition at once thrifty and delicious.
The steak weight is the trimmed weight, after all the fat and sinew has been removed.

PANFRIED STEAK
2 cloves garlic
1 teaspoon cracked black pepper
600g (1lb 5oz) eye fillet steak
    in one piece
3 tablespoons olive oil

BASIL VINAIGRETTE
100ml (3 1/2 fl oz) extra virgin
    olive oil
3 tablespoons sherry vinegar
15 basil leaves
salt and freshly ground
    black pepper

**OLIVE, ROCKET, TOMATO
AND BREAD SALAD**
1 clove garlic
4 tablespoons olive oil
1/2 French loaf, ripped into
    bite-sized pieces
16 black olives
5 medium-sized vine-ripened
    tomatoes, sliced
2 handfuls rocket leaves

Preheat the oven to 190°C (375°F). Peel and crush the garlic. Rub the garlic and pepper all over the piece of steak. Heat the olive oil for the steak in a frying pan until hot but not smoking and brown the piece of steak all over.

Transfer to the oven and finish cooking, turning frequently, about 15 minutes for medium rare. Remove from the oven and let it rest in a warm place for 10 minutes, then slice thinly.

Put all the ingredients for the basil vinaigrette into a food processor or blender and blend until smooth. Season the vinaigrette with salt and pepper to taste.

Peel and finely chop the garlic. Put the olive oil for the salad, the garlic, French bread and olives into a roasting dish and mix well. Place in the oven while the steak is cooking and roast the bread until it is crisp and golden all over and the olives are hot. Mix the bread occasionally as it cooks. Remove from the oven.

Put the hot bread pieces and olives onto a large platter. Scatter the tomatoes and rocket on top (the rocket will wilt but this is as it should be). Put the sliced steak on top and pour any juices from the steak on as well. Dribble the vinaigrette evenly over everything. Serve immediately.

SERVES 4

Vegetable

When you can turn out even the simplest meal of steamed rice, stirfried vegetables and something like a prawn omelette with side sauces all in the time it takes to cook the rice, everyone will be satisfied and very impressed.

Stirfries

Sliced Steak with Vegetable Fried Rice

Stirfried Green Beans with Minced Pork and Egg Noodles

Stirfried Mussels with Ginger and Snow Peas

Stirfried Provençal Vegetables with Roast Chicken and Wine Vinegar

Stirfried Mushrooms and Broccoli with Spring Onion and Crab Omelette and Steamed Rice

Appetising crunchiness

Stirfried Vegetables with Garlic and Ginger

When vegetables are stirfrying correctly you will hear them loudly frying, you will smell the 'wok aroma' of the food cooking, and you will see the vegetables' colour become vivid and translucent. To be sure they are ready, taste some – they will be very hot, well flavoured and taste cooked but with a pleasant underdone crunchiness.

4 cloves garlic	4 baby bok choy	3 tablespoons peanut oil
1 carrot	100g (3^{1}/$_{2}$ oz) green beans	1 stick celery, thinly sliced
3cm (1^{1}/$_{2}$ in) piece ginger	1 red capsicum (pepper)	50g (2oz) snow peas
100g (3^{1}/$_{2}$ oz) broccoli florets	2 spring onions	2 tablespoons soy sauce

Peel and slice the garlic and carrot thinly. Peel and slice the ginger very thinly. Cut the broccoli florets (the flower ends without the thick stalk) into bite-sized pieces. Remove the outer leaves from the baby bok choy and split the bok choy into quarters lengthways. Cut the stalk end off the green beans. Core, seed, and thinly slice the red capsicum. Slice the spring onions into 3cm (1^{1}/$_{2}$ in) lengths.

Heat a wok over a high heat. Add the peanut oil and tilt the wok to swirl the oil over the inside surface. Add the garlic, ginger, carrot, broccoli and bok choy.

Stirfry as described in The Rules on the opposite page for 2 minutes, then add the remaining ingredients and stirfry for a further 3–4 minutes until the vegetables are cooked. Serve immediately. **SERVES 4**

Basic Recipe

The Rules

I learned to stirfry standing at the back door of my local Chinese restaurant. There, anyone could see what went on in the kitchen, so I paid attention. I already knew that stirfried vegetables were delicious and a great way to get your vegetable hit for the day, but watching those Chinese chefs using woks made me realise that stirfrying, once the food was cut up, was an amazing way of cooking quickly and feeding a lot of people fast.

Stirfrying needs an efficient heat source and a wok. If you can stirfry properly all you need is the cheapest Chinese steel wok from an Asian shop. When you buy it, it will probably have a coating of machine oil to prevent it rusting. This will come off with very hot water, a scrubbing brush and plenty of detergent.

This type of wok needs to be 'seasoned' to be made ready for cooking. Seasoning creates a smooth surface on the inside of the wok, which discourages food from sticking or having a metallic taste. To season a steel wok, rub the inside all over with paper towels dipped in cooking oil. Heat it slowly for 15 minutes and wipe it out with clean paper towels, which will become discoloured. Repeat the process until the paper towels remain clean. The inside surface will darken, but this is as it should be.

Clean a seasoned wok with a plastic brush and hot soapy water. Never use metal scouring pads or you will remove the seasoned surface so carefully built up. If you do, season it again.

Buy a spade-shaped Chinese wok utensil to use when stirfrying; there is no other utensil as efficient to use with a wok.

The principle behind stirfrying is simple. Food is cut into uniformly sized shapes, usually bite-sized, before being cooked. A small amount of oil is added to a hot wok, swirled over the surface of the wok to create a non-stick surface and the food added – the meat and tough vegetables first, then the other food, finishing with the most delicate.

The wok is kept very hot and the food is pushed and turned over the oil-coated surface of the wok until it is hot and cooked, but with the vegetables retaining an appetising 'crunchiness'. Stirfrying like this rarely takes more than 5 minutes, so once the food is prepared, a meal can be made very quickly. Stirfried food needs to be served immediately or it will become greasy and soggy.

Sliced Steak with Vegetable Fried Rice

This is a good way to use up leftover rice that might have gone a bit dry in the fridge. Just-cooked rice is too sticky for frying, so if you do cook the rice especially, give it time to cool completely. Two operations go on in this dish: steak is panfried in a piece, then finished in the oven while you cook the rice. If you get organised first, this is a breeze. The steak weight is the trimmed weight, after all the fat and sinew has been removed. Eye fillet, rump and sirloin are all suitable cuts.

See also: *the Basic Recipe for rice, page 110.*

STEAK
1 tablespoon fresh ginger juice
2 cloves garlic
3 tablespoons sesame oil
1 teaspoon sugar
600g (1lb 5oz) piece steak
2 tablespoons toasted
   sesame seeds

VEGETABLE FRIED RICE
4 spring onions
1/2 red capsicum (pepper)
75g (3oz) green beans
2 cloves garlic
4 tablespoons peanut oil
1 tablespoon finely chopped
   fresh ginger

100g (31/2 oz) sliced button
   mushrooms
300g (101/2 oz) raw long grain
   white rice, or 500g (1lb 2oz)
   leftover cooked white rice
1/2 teaspoon salt
1 handful thinly sliced
   iceberg lettuce

Make the ginger juice by finely grating fresh ginger and then squeezing out the juice. Peel the garlic and crush to a paste. Preheat the oven to 190°C (375°F).

Mix the sesame oil, sugar, garlic, and ginger juice together and rub it all over the steak.

Heat a frying pan until hot and add the steak and the flavourings. Brown the steak all over and then put it in the oven for 15 minutes for medium rare steak. Turn it frequently. Remove from the oven and let it rest in a warm place for 10 minutes, then slice thinly.

Cut the spring onions into 1cm (1/2 in) slices, keeping the white parts and green parts in separate piles. Core, seed and thinly slice the capsicum. Trim the ends off the green beans and cut into 1cm (1/2 in) slices. Peel and finely chop the garlic.

If you are cooking the rice for this recipe, prepare it as described in the Basic Recipe on page 110 and let it cool completely.

Heat the wok until very hot. Add the peanut oil and tilt the wok to swirl the oil over the inside surface. Add the garlic, the white part of the spring onions and the ginger and stirfry for 30 seconds.

Add the capsicum, beans and mushrooms and stirfry for 3 minutes until the vegetables are tender but crunchy. Add the rice and salt, mix well and stirfry until hot. If the rice sticks, dribble a little more peanut oil into the wok. Add the lettuce and spring onion greens, and mix well.

Serve the sliced steak on the fried rice with the toasted sesame seeds sprinkled on top. Serve with soy and chilli sauces in small bowls on the side.

SERVES 4

Stirfried Green Beans with Minced Pork and Egg Noodles

This is my take on a dish I once ate in Vietnam. I didn't see it being cooked, so it is an approximation. It is a crunchy dish, which has clear, robust flavours offset with the tang of lime juice and is a favourite in our house.

See also:
Panfried Fish with Stirfried Bok Choy on Egg Noodles, page 134.

350g (12½ oz) thin Chinese egg noodles

300g (10½ oz) green beans
8 cloves garlic

3 tablespoons soy bean oil
2 fresh red chillies, thinly sliced
400g (14oz) lean minced pork
1 tablespoon sugar
3 tablespoons fish sauce

2 tablespoons fresh lime juice
75g (3oz) unsalted roasted peanuts, coarsely chopped
lime wedges for squeezing

Cook the noodles as described in the recipe on page 134 and drain well. Time this operation so that the noodles are drained, hot and ready for the other ingredients.

Trim the ends off the beans and slice into 2cm (1in) lengths. Peel and finely chop the garlic. Heat a wok over a high heat and add the soy bean oil. Swirl the oil over the inside surface of the wok and add the garlic and chillies. Stirfry for 10 seconds and add the pork, sugar, fish sauce and lime juice.

Stirfry over a high heat until the liquid has evaporated and the pork is frying again and starting to brown.

Add the beans and stirfry for 4 minutes until the beans are tender but crisp.

Serve on the noodles, sprinkled with peanuts, with lime wedges for squeezing on the side. **SERVES 4**

Stirfried Mussels with Ginger and Snow Peas

The liquid released by the mussels turns this into a dish with a rather salty sauce that needs the blandness of rice or noodles to go with it.
Shao Xing Chinese cooking wine is available at Asian shops.

See also: *The Rules for mussels, page 10; the Basic Recipe for rice, page 110; or the Basic Recipe for noodles, page 132.*

24 medium-sized mussels
2 cloves garlic
3 tablespoons peanut oil
1 small red dried chilli, thinly sliced

3cm (1½ in) piece peeled fresh ginger, thinly sliced
1 tablespoon soy sauce
3 tablespoons Shao Xing Chinese cooking wine

2 tablespoons chopped coriander leaves
100g (3½ oz) snow peas

Clean the mussels as described in The Rules on page 10. Peel and finely chop the garlic.

Heat a wok over a high heat. Add the peanut oil and swirl to coat the inside surface with oil. Add the garlic, chilli and ginger and stirfry for 10 seconds.

Add the mussels, soy sauce and Shao Xing wine. Stirfry and as the mussels open transfer them to a warm bowl.

Bring the liquid in the wok to the boil and add the coriander and snow peas. Cook, stirring continuously, for 1 minute, and pour the contents of the wok over the mussels.

Serve immediately with plenty of steamed long grain rice cooked as described in the Basic Recipe on page 110, or thick Chinese noodles cooked as described in the Basic Recipe on page 132. **SERVES 4**

Stirfried Provençal Vegetables with Roast Chicken and Wine Vinegar

Mixing food from different cultures can be an unappetising experience for the unsuspecting diner as it requires a comprehensive knowledge of ingredients and cooking methods to be successful. Good examples of fusion food (which of course are delicious) usually evolve naturally. However, the following dish is a light alternative to the usual olive-oil stewed ratatouille-type Provençal handling of such vegetables.

Have ready enough long grain rice for four people, steamed as in the Basic Recipe on page 110.

See also: *the Basic Recipe for chicken, page 48; and the Basic Recipe for rice, page 110.*

CHICKEN

1 Basic Recipe Roast Chicken with Lemon and Garlic

250ml (9fl oz) well-flavoured liquid chicken stock

3 tablespoons wine vinegar, or to taste

2 tablespoons butter

STIRFRIED PROVENÇAL VEGETABLES

1/2 medium-sized eggplant (aubergine)

1 red capsicum (pepper)

4 cloves garlic

1 red onion

3 tablespoons olive oil

1 large sprig fresh thyme

3 courgettes (zucchini), thinly sliced

12 black olives

12 cherry tomatoes

2 tablespoons chopped flat-leafed parsley

50ml (2fl oz) dry white wine

salt and freshly ground black pepper

Roast a chicken as described in the Basic Recipe on page 48, but do not make the gravy. Transfer the chicken to a platter and keep it warm.

Skim the fat off the liquid in the roasting dish with a large spoon. Add the chicken stock and wine vinegar – add more if you like a sharper, sourer result. Bring to the boil and reduce until just becoming syrupy. Add the butter and mix well. Remove from the heat and pour over the chicken.

Cut the eggplant into 2cm (1in) cubes, sprinkle with salt, lightly weight with a couple of plates and leave to drain for 20 minutes. Rinse well and dry with paper towels.

Core, seed and thinly slice the capsicum.

Peel and finely chop the garlic. Peel and thinly slice the red onion.

Heat a wok over a high heat and add the olive oil. Swirl the oil to coat the inside surface.

Add the garlic, thyme, red onion, courgettes, eggplant and olives. Stirfry for 4 minutes until the vegetables are tender but still crisp (apart from the eggplant which has been softened by the salting).

Add the capsicum, tomatoes and parsley and stirfry until they are hot. Add the wine, bring to the boil and boil for 20 seconds. Season well with salt and pepper.

Serve the stirfry with the carved chicken on rice. I like it with Tabasco sauce on the side.

SERVES 4–6

Stirfried Mushrooms and Broccoli with Spring Onion and Crab Omelette and Steamed Rice

Have ready enough steamed rice for four people, cooked as described in the Basic Recipe on page 110. Chinese mushrooms (cloud, oyster and shiitake mushrooms) are all suitable for this dish.

SPRING ONION AND CRAB OMELETTE

3 spring onions
150g (5oz) canned crab meat
3 tablespoons peanut oil
6 eggs, lightly beaten
2 tablespoons soy sauce

MUSHROOMS AND BROCCOLI

100g (3 1/2 oz) broccoli florets
3 cloves garlic
4 tablespoons peanut oil
3cm (1 1/2 in) piece fresh ginger, thinly sliced

250g (9oz) cultivated button mushrooms, sliced
250g (9oz) other cultivated mushrooms
4 tablespoons oyster sauce

See also: the Basic Recipe for omelette, page 18.

Slice the spring onions into 1cm (1/2 in) lengths. Drain and crumble the crab meat.

Heat the peanut oil over a moderate heat in a frying pan and add the spring onions. Fry them, without browning, for 20 seconds, then add the eggs and cook as described in the Basic Recipe on page 18. Omit the herbs but instead add the soy sauce and crab meat. Fold the omelette in half and transfer to a wooden board to cool.

When cool, slice the omelette into 1cm (1/2 in) thick slices.

Cut the broccoli florets (the flower ends without the thick stalk) into bite-sized pieces. Peel and thinly slice the garlic.

Heat a wok until hot, add the peanut oil and tilt the wok to swirl the oil over the inside surface. Add the garlic, ginger and broccoli and stirfry for 2 minutes. Add the mushrooms and stirfry for 3 minutes until the broccoli is tender but crunchy and the mushrooms are soft. Add the oyster sauce and mix well, stirfrying until everything is hot.

Serve the stirfry with the rice, and garnish with the sliced omelette. Have chilli and soy sauces in small bowls on the side for dipping.

SERVES 4

Stirfried Mushrooms and Broccoli with Spring Onion and Crab Omelette and Steamed Rice

Meltingly tender

Roast Chicken

The sublime aroma of chicken roasting absolutely epitomises home cooking – and once you know how to cook it so the white meat is tender and the skin crisp and golden, you can go on to create many other dishes.

Alexander's Roast Chicken on
  Potato Gratin
Spiced Roast Chicken Salad
Roast Chicken with Tomatoes and
  Anchovies and Herbed Spaghetti
Sweet Soy and Ginger Chicken with
  Stirfried Noodles and Peanuts
Roast Chicken with Pumpkin,
  Couscous and Herbed Yoghurt

Roast Chicken with Lemon and Garlic

The wing tips of the chicken have no meat on them, so cut them off as they tend to burn.

4 large cloves garlic
1.4 kg (3lb) organic chicken,
   wing tips cut off
1 lemon, halved

250ml (9fl oz) water
1/2 teaspoon salt
1/2 teaspoon freshly ground
   black pepper

250ml (9fl oz) well-flavoured
   liquid chicken stock
1 1/2 tablespoons cornflour
2 tablespoons water

Preheat the oven to 190°C (375°F). Peel the garlic and flatten it gently with the side of a knife.

Put the chicken into a roasting dish just big enough to hold it. Squeeze the lemon over the chicken and put the squeezed halves and the garlic inside it. Pin the body cavity closed with a short bamboo skewer. Turn the chicken onto its breast and add the first measure of water to the pan. Sprinkle with the salt and pepper.

Put the chicken into the oven and roast for 35 minutes, then turn it onto its back and roast for a further 35 minutes until well cooked.

To test for readiness, insert the blade of a small knife between the leg and the breast and check that the juices that run out are clear. Most of the liquid in the bottom of the pan will have evaporated. Transfer the chicken from the pan to a platter and keep it warm.

Skim the fat off the liquid in the roasting dish with a large spoon. Add the chicken stock, put the pan over a direct heat and bring to the boil. Mix the cornflour to a paste with the 2 tablespoons of water and whisk into the boiling stock so that it thickens to the consistency of liquid cream. Turn the heat down and simmer for 1 minute. Taste the gravy and season with salt and pepper. Put the gravy into a warm jug. Carve the chicken and discard the lemon and garlic. Serve the chicken with the gravy on the side.

SERVES 4–6

The Rules

The idea in roasting chicken is to have the inside cooked at the same time as the skin crisps and turns a delectable golden brown.
Roasting the chicken with water in the pan ensures a moist bird and also plenty of caramelised juices left after the water has evaporated during cooking. These juices can be used for the gravy.

Don't worry about the correct way to carve. Use a sharp knife and slice off anything obvious and easy to slice, then just pull and cut the bird apart without shredding it. The chicken should be well cooked enough to make this easy.

Alexander's Roast Chicken on Potato Gratin

My son Alexander's favourite meal and the ultimate comfort food – roast chicken stuffed with bread, herbs and yoghurt, which gives the stuffing a lemony taste as well as keeping everything moist. This dish can easily do duty as a family meal or as the main part of a special meal. In the unlikely event of any being left over, it is equally delicious cold the next day.

The gratin is the simplest sort and is perfect with stuffed chicken – it involves roasting vegetables without much fat and keeping them covered throughout cooking. The potatoes are flavoured with herbs, olive oil and cook in their own steam. Drying the potato slices is a labour of love that makes sure they stick together.

See also: *the Basic Recipe for salad, page 28.*

STUFFING

3 cloves garlic

1 tablespoon fresh thyme leaves

4 tablespoons chopped
    flat-leafed parsley

2 tablespoons extra virgin olive oil

125ml (4fl oz) natural yoghurt

1 teaspoon Maldon sea salt

1/2 teaspoon freshly ground black
    pepper

2 rashers rindless bacon,
    finely chopped

200g (7oz) finely crumbled stale
    bread of your choice

CHICKEN

1.4 kg (3lb) organic chicken,
    wing tips cut off

250ml (9fl oz) water

250ml (9fl oz) dry white wine

2 tablespoons butter

POTATO GRATIN

900g (2lb) waxy potatoes

1 fresh bay leaf

2 cloves garlic

3 tablespoons extra virgin olive oil

salt and freshly ground
    black pepper

Peel and finely chop the garlic. Mix all the ingredients for the stuffing together well (I usually do it with my hands) so that they form a sticky ball of stuffing. Taste it (it is delicious) to check the seasoning.

Preheat the oven to 190°C (375°F). Push the stuffing into the chicken's body cavity. Close the cavity by pulling the skin together and pinning it with a bamboo skewer. Put the chicken in a roasting dish just big enough to hold it, breast down. Pour in the water and roast for 45 minutes. Turn the chicken onto its back and roast for a further 45 minutes, basting occasionally. The chicken will be golden brown and the stuffing hot right through to the middle. Test by pushing the blade of a small knife into the middle of the stuffing, leave it there for 20 seconds, remove and carefully feel it with your fingertips. If it is cooked it will be almost too hot to touch. Transfer the chicken to a warm platter. Skim the fat off the pan juices and add the wine. Bring to the boil and boil until the mixture is becoming syrupy. Stir in the butter and remove from the heat.

Scrub the potatoes well, cut into 1/2 cm (1/4 in) thick slices, and dry each slice on a clean cloth. Pack the potato slices in tight rows into a small casserole or deep oven dish just big enough to hold them. Peel and chop the garlic. Put the bay leaf and garlic on top and dribble the extra virgin olive oil over everything. Season well with salt and pepper. Cover tightly and bake for 1 hour (at the same time the chicken is roasting) until the potatoes are tender and fragrant.

Serve each person some of the chicken and stuffing on a portion of the potatoes with a little white wine sauce on top. A green salad is all that is needed to complete the meal. See the Basic Recipe on page 28. **SERVES 4–6**

Spiced Roast Chicken Salad

A roast chicken makes an excellent hot salad, perfect for lunch with crusty bread. Here it is flavoured with aromatic Indian spices, the gravy is dispensed with and the chicken served as part of an untossed salad with lime vinaigrette. As it roasts, the chicken fills your kitchen with all the fragrance of an Indian spice market. Don't worry about tossing the salad; it would just end up looking over-handled and messy. Better to let it get mixed as people help themselves to it.

SPICED ROAST CHICKEN
5 cloves garlic
5cm (2in) long piece peeled fresh
　ginger, chopped
1/2 cinnamon stick, broken up
1 teaspoon cardamom seeds,
　coarsely ground
1/2 teaspoon cracked black pepper
2 teaspoons ground turmeric

2 small dried red chillies, chopped
50ml (2fl oz) olive oil
1.4 kg (3lb) organic chicken,
　wing tips cut off
100ml (3 1/2 fl oz) water

SALAD
1/2 cucumber
1 red onion

1 Cos lettuce, leaves detached
　from the stem
150g (5oz) cherry tomatoes, halved
2 tablespoons chopped coriander
150ml (5fl oz) extra virgin olive oil
grated zest of 1 lime
50ml (2fl oz) fresh lime juice
salt and freshly ground
　black pepper

See also: the Basic Recipe for chicken, page 48.

Peel and chop the garlic. Put the garlic, ginger, cinnamon, cardamom, cracked black pepper, turmeric, chillies and the 50ml olive oil into a food processor and blend until smooth. Pour and spread the mixture evenly all over the chicken, inside and out. Set aside to marinate for 30 minutes. Preheat the oven to 190°C (375°F).

Put the chicken into a roasting dish breast down, add the water and roast as described in the Basic Recipe on page 48. The water will evaporate.

Peel the cucumber and cut it into small, bite-sized chunks. Peel and thinly slice the red onion. Make a bed of the Cos lettuce leaves on a large platter.

Carve the hot chicken or simply pull it apart and put it tidily onto the lettuce. Scatter the cucumber, tomatoes, onion and coriander on top.

Mix the extra virgin olive oil, lime zest and juice together well and season with salt and pepper to taste. Pour the dressing evenly over everything and serve.　　　　**SERVES 6**

Spiced Roast Chicken Salad

Roast Chicken with Tomatoes and Anchovies and Herbed Spaghetti

Here a chicken is roasted on a mixture of tomatoes and anchovies that cook down into a sauce. Don't be afraid of the anchovies; they lose their fishiness and give a salty, savoury taste to the dish. The herbed spaghetti is a simple treatment of pasta that relies on using good pasta and olive oil, and cooking it carefully.

CHICKEN WITH TOMATOES AND ANCHOVIES

1 onion
2 cloves garlic
3 tablespoons extra virgin olive oil
8 anchovy fillets, chopped
1 tablespoon sugar
400g (14oz) can Italian tomatoes in juice, mashed
100ml (3½ fl oz) well-flavoured liquid chicken stock
½ teaspoon salt
½ teaspoon cracked black pepper
1.4 kg (3lb) organic chicken, wing tips cut off
2 tablespoons chopped flat-leafed parsley

HERBED SPAGHETTI

400g (14oz) Italian dried spaghetti
2 cloves garlic
finely grated zest of 1 lemon
3 tablespoons extra virgin olive oil
3 tablespoons finely chopped flat-leafed parsley
10 basil leaves, ripped into small pieces
salt and freshly ground black pepper

Preheat the oven to 190°C (375°F). Peel and thinly slice the onion. Peel and finely chop the garlic. Heat the first measure of extra virgin olive oil in a frying pan over a moderate heat. Gently fry the onion and garlic, without browning, until soft. Mix the anchovies, sugar, tomatoes, chicken stock, salt and pepper with the onions and put into a deep roasting dish. Put the chicken on top, breast side down, and push it down into the mixture.

Roast for 35 minutes, turn the chicken onto its back and roast for a further 35 minutes. Add a little stock or water if the tomato mixture becomes dry during cooking.

Remove from the oven and put the chicken on a warm platter. Skim the fat off the tomato mixture, which will now have become a thick sauce. Pour the sauce over the chicken. Sprinkle with the parsley.

Cook the spaghetti as described in the Basic Recipe on page 122. The length of time depends on the thickness of the spaghetti, but about 10–12 minutes usually does it. I always taste it and feel it as I bite a piece. Drain and put into a warm bowl. Peel and finely chop the garlic. Add the remaining ingredients, seasoning well with salt and pepper, and mix well.

Carve the chicken. Serve each person some pasta with chicken and sauce on top.

SERVES 4–6

See also: the Basic Recipe for pasta, page 122.

Sweet Soy and Ginger Chicken with Stirfried Noodles and Peanuts

A very untraditional mix of Chinese flavours gives this roast chicken an Asian spin. The chicken is roasted in the usual manner but with a flavouring mix in the bottom of the pan, which is brushed onto it as it cooks. This results in a shiny, lacquered chicken of a deep mahogany colour. Watch carefully as you repeatedly paint the chicken with the sweet soy while it cooks so that you can achieve just the right 'varnished' look to it.
Simple, tasty stirfried noodles go well with chicken.

SWEET SOY AND GINGER CHICKEN
5 cloves garlic
5cm (2in) piece fresh ginger, sliced
1.4 kg (3lb) organic chicken, wing tips cut off
2 tablespoons sesame oil
125ml (4fl oz) light soy sauce
4 tablespoons sugar
1/4 teaspoon Chinese five spice powder
100ml (3 1/2 fl oz) water

STIRFRIED NOODLES AND PEANUTS
350g (12 1/2 oz) thick egg noodles
3 tablespoons peanut oil
4 spring onions
1 clove garlic
1 tablespoon finely chopped fresh ginger
2 tablespoons chopped coriander
4 tablespoons chopped unsalted roasted peanuts
2 tablespoons sesame oil
cucumber slices and tomato wedges for garnish

Preheat the oven to 190°C (375°F). Peel the garlic and flatten it gently with the side of a knife. Put the ginger and garlic inside the chicken and pin it closed with a skewer. Put the chicken into a roasting dish just big enough to hold it.

Mix the sesame oil, soy sauce, sugar, five spice powder and water and pour it over the chicken. Turn the chicken onto its breast and put it into the oven. Roast for 35 minutes then turn the chicken onto its back and roast for a further 35 minutes.

As the chicken cooks, dip a wide pastry brush into the liquid in the bottom of the pan then brush it over the chicken so that it is coated all over. Do this frequently during the whole cooking time and you will build up a flavoursome, shiny coating all over the chicken. If the mixture in the bottom of the pan gets too dry and starts to burn, add a little water.

When the chicken is cooked, remove it from the oven and keep it warm. Discard the liquid at the bottom of the roasting dish, the bamboo skewer and the garlic and ginger inside the chicken.

Cook the noodles in plenty of boiling water as described in the Basic Recipe on page 132. Drain well, add the peanut oil and toss to prevent the noodles sticking together.

Slice the spring onions into 3cm (1 1/4 in) pieces. Peel and finely chop the garlic.

Heat a wok until hot and add the noodles, spring onions, garlic and ginger, and quickly stirfry until the noodles are hot again. Add the coriander, peanuts and sesame oil, toss well and put the noodles onto a large warm platter.

Carve the chicken and put it on top of the noodles. Scatter the cucumber and tomato around the chicken. Serve with soy and sweet chilli sauce in small bowls on the side.

SERVES 4–6

See also: the Basic Recipe for noodles, page 132.

Roast Chicken with Pumpkin, Couscous and Herbed Yoghurt

While it may look complicated, this is merely a combination of four simple recipes. The intense sweetness of the roasted pumpkin, the savoury fragrance of the chicken, the smokiness of the paprika-flavoured couscous and the tartness of the yoghurt add up to a dish that looks stunning and is great for a special dinner.

Make sure the cooked pumpkin is a deep orange colour and slightly shrivelled so that all its sweetness is concentrated.

See also: the Basic Recipe for chicken, page 48; and the Basic Recipe for salad, page 28.

CHICKEN

1 Basic Recipe Roast Chicken with Lemon and Garlic

PUMPKIN

900g (2lb) skinned, seeded pumpkin
3 tablespoons olive oil
1 teaspoon cumin seeds
2 small dried red chillies, finely sliced
salt and freshly ground black pepper

COUSCOUS

250g (9oz) instant couscous
1 tablespoon extra virgin olive oil
1 teaspoon smoked sweet Spanish paprika
grated zest of 1 lemon
salt and freshly ground black pepper
boiling water

HERBED YOGHURT

1 clove garlic
250ml (9fl oz) plain unsweetened yoghurt
a small handful each of parsley, mint and coriander sprigs
salt and freshly ground black pepper

GARNISH

coriander leaves
grated zest of 1 lemon
black olives

Roast the chicken as described in the Basic Recipe on page 48, but omit the gravy. Carve the chicken and keep it warm.

While the chicken is cooking, make the pumpkin, couscous and yoghurt.

Preheat the oven to 190°C (375°F). Cut the pumpkin into large, bite-sized pieces. Put the olive oil, pumpkin, cumin seeds and chillies into a small roasting dish and mix well, seasoning with salt and pepper to taste. Place in the oven and roast for 45 minutes to 1 hour until the pumpkin is well cooked.

Put the couscous, extra virgin olive oil, paprika and lemon zest into a heatproof bowl. Season with salt and pepper and mix well. Add enough boiling water to cover the couscous, quickly mix again, cover tightly with tinfoil and set aside in a warm place for 25–30 minutes.

Uncover and fluff the couscous up with a fork, making sure there are no lumps. The couscous will still be hot.

Peel and chop the garlic. Put the yoghurt, herbs and garlic into a food processor and process until smooth. Season to taste. Set aside.

To serve, put the hot couscous onto a large, warm serving platter. Put the carved chicken on top and scatter the hot pumpkin over the chicken. Dribble the herbed yoghurt over the top of everything and garnish with the coriander leaves, lemon zest and black olives. Present the couscous platter at the table and let everyone help themselves. A green salad is the only accompaniment needed – see the Basic Recipe on page 28.

SERVES 4–6

Juicy tenderness

Panfried Steak

A steak that is tender, succulent and cooked exactly to the degree you like can form the foundation of many great meals. While some people nowadays shy away from large pieces of red meat, thinly sliced lean steak can be a delicious part of Asian dishes, sandwiches and hot salads.

Panfried Sirloin Steak with
    Red Onions
Minute Steak Sandwich with
    Roasted Vegetables and Aïoli
Teriyaki Eye Fillet with Roasted
    Eggplant Salad
Vietnamese-style Steak with Rice,
    Vegetables and Dipping Sauce
Panfried Rump Steak with Potato
    and Rocket Stew
Spice-rubbed Lamb Short Loins
    with Roasted Kumara and
    Fresh Mint Chutney

Panfried Eye Fillet with Pan Juices and Wholegrain Mustard

Panfried eye fillet with the juices from the pan, a dollop of wholegrain mustard, a crunchy green salad and a piece of chewy sourdough bread to wipe the plate with is a meal that can go anywhere. It is simple, elegant and delicious and can do duty as a quick everyday meal or as something special for guests. This recipe will work just as well using any type of steak. The steak weight is the trimmed weight, after all the fat and sinew has been removed.

2 cloves garlic
3 tablespoons olive oil

4 x 200g (7oz) slices eye fillet
freshly ground black pepper
150ml (5fl oz) red wine

1 tablespoon butter
4 tablespoons wholegrain mustard

Peel the garlic and crush to a paste. Mix the olive oil and garlic and pour them over the pieces of eye fillet, mixing well so that all the meat is well covered. Sprinkle with plenty of freshly ground black pepper. Set aside for 10 minutes.

Heat a heavy frying pan until very hot, so that a drop of water dropped into it immediately turns into a boiling bead of moisture and evaporates. Add the steak and all of the oil and garlic.

Panfry the steaks on each side until cooked the way you like them, using the touch test to tell when they are ready. Transfer the steak from the pan to a plate and keep it warm.

Pour any oil out of the pan and put the pan back onto high heat. Add the wine and scrape the pan with a wooden spoon to dislodge any caramelised meat juices in the pan. This is called deglazing.

Bring the wine to the boil and boil until it starts to become syrupy. Add any juices that have seeped onto the plate from the steak. Stir the butter in quickly and remove from the heat.

Serve the steak with a little of the sauce and a tablespoon of mustard on each piece.

SERVES 4

The Rules

The term steak means cuts of beef that are of uniform thickness and can be quickly cooked by panfrying, barbecuing or grilling. These include rump, sirloin (or porterhouse), scotch fillet (or rib-eye or cube roll), skirt steak and eye fillet (or tenderloin). Though it is the most expensive cut, eye fillet is my favourite as it is very tender and not too strongly flavoured. When buying, look for beef that is a vivid, shiny red.

Cooking a steak the way you like it can be daunting for many people, as cooking times will depend on the thickness of the piece of steak. This is where your sense of touch comes in. If you give a rare steak a deliberate prod with your forefinger (do it quickly and you will not get burnt) it should be soft to the touch and an indentation will be left. Medium rare steaks are still soft but spring back. Medium feels firm with a definite spring-back feel, and well done is very firm, bordering on hard to the touch.

You may not get it right the first few times, but if you persevere you will soon be able to tell when a steak is cooked the way you like it by giving it a quick prod. If in doubt, undercook it; you can always put it back on the heat and cook it some more.

The look of a steak is also important. It should have a caramelised dark brown colour that looks crisp and crusty. This appearance is achieved by cooking steak in a hot pan or on a hot grill or barbecue.

If the pan or grill is not kept hot, the steak will stew in its own juices, which should be avoided. If you are going to slice the steak after it is cooked, you need to let it rest in a warm place for 5–10 minutes before cutting it, otherwise its juices will run out, leaving the meat dry.

Panfried Sirloin Steak with Red Onions

Here the classic combination of steak and onions is given a modern twist. Great with fried or mashed floury potatoes and a salad to follow.

Don't try to hurry the initial frying of the onions if you want them to have a cooked texture and a good flavour. The lemon juice will quickly evaporate, but not before reacting with the onions and keeping them a delightful pink rather than the depressing grey which would result if lemon juice was not used.

The sirloin steak weight is the trimmed weight, after all the fat and sinew has been removed.

5 tablespoons olive oil
2 cloves garlic
5 large red onions
1 large sprig fresh thyme
juice of 1/2 lemon

4 x 150g (5oz) pieces sirloin steak, cut across the grain
125ml (4fl oz) red wine
250ml (9fl oz) well-flavoured liquid beef stock

salt and freshly ground black pepper
4 x 2cm (1in) thick slices French loaf, cut on the diagonal
1 clove garlic, peeled

See also: The Rules for steak, page 59; and the Basic Recipe for stew, page 98.

Heat a frying pan over a moderate heat and add 3 tablespoons of the olive oil.

Peel and finely chop the garlic. Peel and thinly slice the onions. Add the finely chopped garlic, thyme, onions and lemon juice, mix well and gently fry, without browning, until the onions are soft, as described in the Basic Recipe on page 98. Remove the onions from the pan, put them into a bowl and set aside.

Clean the pan, put it on high heat and add the remaining 2 tablespoons of olive oil. When the oil is hot but not smoking, add the pieces of steak and cook them the way you like them, testing their doneness with the touch test, as described in The Rules on page 59. Transfer the steak from the pan to a plate and keep warm.

Pour the oil from the pan and discard. Put the pan over a moderate heat and add the onion mixture. When it is hot add the wine and stock, bring to the boil and scrape the pan with a wooden spoon. Boil until the mixture is thick and syrupy. Taste and season with salt and pepper.

Toast the French bread and rub each piece on one side with the clove of peeled garlic.

Sit each steak on a slice of toast and spoon some of the onion mix on top.   **SERVES 4**

Panfried Sirloin Steak with Red Onions

Minute Steak Sandwich with Roasted Vegetables and Aïoli

The word 'minute' refers to the time it takes to cook the steak, not the size of the sandwich!
When making the aïoli (garlic mayonnaise), pay special attention to what happens because it is an emulsion, which must be done carefully.
The steak weight is the trimmed weight, after all the fat and sinew has been removed.

2 courgettes (zucchini)
1 carrot
12 green beans
8 thin slices peeled,
    seeded pumpkin
3 tablespoons olive oil
salt and freshly ground
    black pepper

4 x 15cm (6in) pieces French
    bread, split in half lengthways
1 handful rocket leaves
2 tablespoons olive oil
4 x ½ cm (¼ in) thick slices rump
    or sirloin, about 10cm (4in) long
    and 5cm (2in) wide or use
    8 smaller slices

AÏOLI
2 egg yolks
2 cloves garlic, peeled and crushed
    to a paste
200ml (7fl oz) extra virgin olive oil
salt

Preheat the oven to 200°C (400°F). Trim the ends off the courgettes and thinly slice lengthways. Peel the carrot and thinly slice lengthways. Trim the stalk ends off the beans.

Put the courgettes, carrot, beans and pumpkin into a wide, shallow baking tray, add the first measure of the olive oil and season well with salt and pepper. Toss so that the vegetables are coated with oil.

Bake in a hot oven until the vegetables are tender to the bite and look browned and slightly shrivelled, about 20 minutes. Remove from the oven and keep warm.

While the vegetables are roasting, make the aïoli. Whisk the egg yolks and garlic in a food processor or in a bowl with a whisk, until well mixed.

Start adding the extra virgin olive oil, drop by drop, processing or stirring continuously. When you see the mixture start to thicken and look creamy (not grainy and thin), start adding the oil in a very thin trickle. Stir or process continuously until all the oil is used and the

mixture is thick and buttery. Taste and season with salt and set aside.

If the mixture refuses to thicken and is grainy and thin, it means you have added the oil too quickly, but you can fix it. Pour the curdled mixture into a bowl and set it aside. Completely clean the processor bowl or the bowl you were working in. Get a fresh egg yolk and the remaining oil (or more oil) and start again, this time adding the oil very slowly. Once you see the mixture thicken as it should, then start adding the curdled mixture slowly, stirring continuously until it is all incorporated.

Spread the tops and bottoms of the French bread with plenty of aïoli and put some rocket leaves on the bottom halves.

Heat the remaining 2 tablespoons of olive oil in a frying pan until hot but not smoking. Sear each piece of steak for about 15 seconds on each side and put a piece of hot steak (or 2 if you are using 2 per sandwich) on top of the rocket. Pile some roasted vegetables on top and finish with the top piece of bread. Serve immediately.

SERVES 4

Teriyaki Eye Fillet with Roasted Eggplant Salad

A warm roasted vegetable salad connects with Japanese-flavoured panfried steak to give a dish of two layers that has a balance of sweet, salty and sour flavours.
Sake is Japanese rice wine and mirin is sweet Japanese rice cooking wine.
The steak weight is the trimmed weight, after all the fat and sinew has been removed.

EGGPLANT SALAD
2 medium-sized eggplants (aubergines)
1 spring onion
2 tablespoons sesame seeds
4 tablespoons soy bean oil

4 tablespoons sesame oil
juice of 1 lemon
4 lemon wedges

TERIYAKI EYE FILLET
2 tablespoons soy bean oil

400g (14oz) eye fillet, sliced into 8 equal slices
4 tablespoons sake
4 tablespoons mirin
4 tablespoons dark soy sauce

See also: the Basic Recipe for rice, page 110.

Toast the sesame seeds in a dry pan until just beginning to darken. Preheat the oven to 200°C (400°F). Cut the eggplant into slices 1cm ($^1/_2$ in) thick. Thinly slice the spring onion on the diagonal.

Mix the soy bean and sesame oils together well and paint the eggplant slices liberally with them. Put the eggplant slices in one layer on a large flat baking sheet. Put into the oven and roast until the underside of the eggplant slices has browned, about 10 minutes. Turn the eggplant over and roast until the other side is brown.

Transfer from the oven to a serving platter, leaving room for the eye fillet. Sprinkle with the lemon juice, spring onion and sesame seeds and put the lemon wedges on the side.

Heat the 2 tablespoons of soy bean oil over a high heat until hot but not smoking. Add the slices of eye fillet to the pan and cook until well browned on each side but still rare. Sprinkle the sake evenly over the steak and cook for 15 seconds. Remove the steak from the pan and keep it warm.

Add the mirin and soy sauce to the pan and bring to the boil. Put the steak and any juices from it back into the pan and quickly coat the steak with the sauce.

Transfer the steak to the space on the platter and pour the sauce over it. Serve it with steamed short grain white rice as described in the Basic Recipe on page 110.

SERVES 4

Vietnamese-style Steak with Rice, Vegetables and Dipping Sauce

Panfried marinated steak, fluffy steamed rice, crunchy raw vegetables and sweet and sour spicy dipping sauce – four simple operations put together to make a meal of texture and flavour contrasts that is a favourite in our house. Excellent food for when the weather is hot and the appetite jaded.

The steak weight is the trimmed weight, after all the fat and sinew has been removed.

The simple dipping sauce is the quintessential Vietnamese condiment. It has sweet (sugar), sour (lime juice), salty (fish sauce) and hot (chilli) flavours so it needs to be tasted carefully to make sure that the four flavours are balanced.

See also: *The Rules for steak, page 59; and the Basic Recipe for rice, page 110.*

STEAK

1 stalk lemongrass

2 cloves garlic

2 tablespoons fish sauce

1 teaspoon sugar

500g (1lb 2oz) sirloin steak, in one piece

3 tablespoons peanut oil

RICE

400g (14oz) long grain white rice

500ml (18fl oz) water

VEGETABLES

raw carrot sticks

cucumber slices

tomato wedges

basil and mint leaves

DIPPING SAUCE

1 clove garlic

3 tablespoons sugar, or to taste

100ml (3$1/2$ fl oz) fish sauce

100ml (3$1/2$ fl oz) fresh lime juice

1 small dried red chilli, finely sliced

Discard the coarse outer leaves of the lemongrass and use the bulbous end only, squashed with the side of a knife. Peel the garlic and crush to a paste.

Mix the lemongrass, garlic, fish sauce, sugar and steak together and set aside to marinate for 1 hour, covered, in the refrigerator. Turn the meat occasionally. Remove the meat from the marinade and discard the lemongrass. Dry the steak on paper towels.

Heat the peanut oil in a frying pan over a moderate heat and add the steak. Brown on all sides and cook over a moderate heat, being careful not to burn it, for 10–15 minutes until medium rare (or longer if you like it more cooked). Test with the touch test as described in The Rules on page 59.

Remove from the pan, let it rest for 10 minutes in a warm place then slice thinly across the grain of the meat.

Prepare and cook the rice as described in the Basic Recipe on page 110.

Prepare enough raw vegetables for four people.

Peel and finely slice the garlic for the dipping sauce. Mix all the sauce ingredients together, stirring until the sugar has dissolved. Taste and adjust the sweet, sour, salty and hot flavours if necessary. Set aside.

To serve, put the rice into a large bowl. Put the sliced steak onto a platter with the vegetables and herbs. Divide the dipping sauce into four small bowls. Give everyone a pair of chopsticks and a bowl or plate to fill with rice. Let them help themselves to the steak and vegetables and eat them on the rice, dipping into their small bowls of sauce as they go.

SERVES 4

Panfried Rump Steak with Potato and Rocket Stew

Creamy potatoes stewed with garlic, wine and cream with peppery rocket added at the end make a great accompaniment to panfried steak with wine and pan juices.
Make the stew before cooking the steak, but do not add the rocket or cream until the steak is ready. As with all stews, the frying of the onions and garlic is the 'sofrito' stage and needs to be done without hurrying so that you get maximum flavour from them. The best way to do this is to test some of the onion; it should be completely soft and 'melted' with no resistance to the bite. The rump steak weight is the trimmed weight, after all the fat and sinew has been removed.

See also: *The Rules for steak, page 59.*

POTATO AND ROCKET STEW
900g (2lb) waxy potatoes
2 large onions
6 cloves garlic
3 tablespoons olive oil
125ml (4fl oz) well-flavoured liquid
    chicken stock
125ml (4fl oz) white wine
1 fresh bay leaf
1 teaspoon salt
1/2 teaspoon freshly ground
    white pepper
150g (5oz) rocket leaves
125ml (4fl oz) cream

RUMP STEAK
2 cloves garlic
3 tablespoons olive oil
4 x 150g (5oz) slices rump steak
freshly ground black pepper
150ml (5fl oz) red wine
1 tablespoon butter

Peel the potatoes and cut into 2cm (1in) cubes. Peel and finely chop the onions and garlic.

Heat the olive oil in a heavy saucepan over a moderate heat and add the onions, potatoes and garlic. Sauté, without browning, until the onion is soft and transparent.

Add the stock, wine, bay leaf, salt and pepper, mix well and bring to the boil. Simmer for 40–45 minutes until everything is tender and the mixture is thick. Stir in the rocket leaves and cream and let the rocket wilt.

Peel and crush the garlic for the steak to a paste. Mix the olive oil and garlic and pour over the slices of rump, mixing well so that the steak is well covered. Sprinkle with plenty of freshly ground black pepper. Set aside for 10 minutes.

Heat a heavy frying pan until very hot and add the slices of rump and all of the olive oil and garlic. Panfry the steak on each side until cooked the way you like it, using the touch test as described in The Rules on page 59 to tell when it is ready. Transfer the steak from the pan to a plate and keep warm.

Pour any oil out of the pan and put the pan back onto high heat. Add the wine and scrape the pan with a wooden spoon to dislodge any caramelised meat juices in the pan. Bring the wine to the boil and boil until it starts to become syrupy. Add any juices that have seeped onto the plate from the steak. Stir the butter in quickly and remove from the heat.

Serve a slice of steak on a large spoonful of the stew. Pour the red wine sauce over the steak.

SERVES 4

Spice-rubbed Lamb Short Loins with Roasted Kumara and Fresh Mint Chutney

Lamb short loins can be panfried just like steak. A rectangular cut of boneless lamb, they cook quickly and are very tender. The sweetness of kumara (sweet potato) is intensified by roasting and goes well with spicy lamb and tart mint chutney.

SPICE-RUBBED LAMB
2 cloves garlic
1 teaspoon ground turmeric
2 tablespoons ground cumin
1 tablespoon ground ginger
1/2 teaspoon ground cinnamon
4 tablespoons olive oil
4 lamb short loins, (about 200g or 7oz each) all fat and sinew removed

KUMARA
5 medium-sized kumara (sweet potatoes)
olive oil for brushing
salt and freshly ground black pepper

FRESH MINT CHUTNEY
1 apple
1 large handful mint
juice of 1 lemon
3 tablespoons sugar
1 small fresh green chilli, seeded

See also: The Rules for steak, page 59.

Peel and crush the garlic to a paste. Mix the garlic, turmeric, cumin, ginger, cinnamon and 3 tablespoons of the olive oil for the lamb until you have a paste. Rub the paste all over the lamb. Set aside to marinate for 30 minutes.

Heat a frying pan over a moderate heat and add the remaining tablespoon of olive oil and the lamb. Panfry over a moderate heat, being careful not to burn the spices, for about 4–5 minutes each side for medium, using the touch test as described in The Rules on page 59. Remove from the pan and let it rest in a warm place for 6–8 minutes, then slice thinly.

Preheat the oven to 190°C (375°F). Peel and cut the kumara into 1cm (1/2 in) thick slices lengthways. Brush the kumara slices on each side with olive oil and put them onto a flat baking sheet in one layer (use two sheets if necessary). Sprinkle the slices with salt and pepper and bake for 30–40 minutes until the kumara is tender and browned. Remove from the oven.

Peel, core and slice the apple. Put all the chutney ingredients into a food processor or blender and purée until smooth. Put into a bowl and set aside.

Serve the sliced lamb on the roasted kumara with a dollop of chutney on top.

SERVES 4

Panfried

Fish

A delicate piece of just-cooked panfried fish is the perfect partner to crisp green salads in summer or layered baked potatoes in winter. Following a few simple rules you can produce a sublime meal.

Lemon and Courgette Risotto
  with Panfried Salmon
Panfried Fish with Fresh Herbs,
  Glass Noodles and Dipping Sauce
Panfried Fish with Tomatoes and
  Basil and Baked Potatoes
Panfried Fish with Tomato and
  Ginger Jam and Sticky Rice
Panfried Fish with Roasted
  Capsicum Salad
Escabèched Snapper Salad

Golden perfection

Basic Recipe

Panfried Snapper with Lemon and Capers

This dish has been around restaurant menus forever, but done well at home it is always a winner. Any firm white fish with thickish fillets can be used.

4 x 200g (7oz) pieces skinned, boned snapper fillet, or other firm white fish fillet	plain flour for dusting 4 tablespoons olive oil 2 tablespoons butter juice of 1 large lemon	2 tablespoons capers 1 tablespoon chopped flat-leafed parsley

Preheat the oven to 200°C (400°F). Dust the fish with the flour, shaking off any excess.

Heat the olive oil over a moderate heat and add the fish. You should see and hear it start to fry immediately. Panfry it on both sides over a moderate to high heat until it is golden brown.

Carefully place the fish on an ovenproof serving platter and put it in the oven until it is just cooked. This will depend on the thickness of the fillets. Test by inserting a small knife into the fillet and pulling it to one side. If the knife goes in easily and the flesh breaks, it is ready. After you have cooked fish like this a few times you will find it easy.

Meanwhile pour the oil from the pan and put the pan back over a moderate heat. Add the butter and let it melt and bubble. The pan must not be hot enough to brown the butter.

Add the lemon juice, capers and parsley and gently cook until the mixture thickens slightly. This will take only seconds.

Remove from the heat and spoon the caper mixture over the fish. Serve the hot fish with crusty bread and salad. **SERVES 4**

The Rules

Some of my most memorable meals have simply been panfried fillets of fresh fish – the outside a crispy golden brown and the inside just cooked so that it melts in the mouth – with a crunchy, juicy salad, crusty bread and a cool glass of white wine.

This sort of fish cookery has more affinity with the simple summer food of the Mediterranean than that of the local fish and chip shop. It is a dish easy to get right and one that can form the basis of many special and everyday meals. It is also a dish that demands the cook's full attention.

The fish must be very fresh; frozen fish has no place in a good cook's repertoire. It is easy to co-ordinate a golden exterior with a just-cooked interior by using the chef's trick of finishing the fish in the oven. This is especially practical when panfrying a large amount of fish.

I panfry fish in olive oil because I like the taste and it's healthier too. I fry the fish until it looks the way I want it, then slide it onto an ovenproof dish and let it cook through in the oven. Any firm white fish can be cooked this way. Salmon and tuna can also be cooked like this but are much better left medium rare, even if you do have to explain to more conservative guests that you meant to leave it raw in the middle.

Firm white fish that panfry well include John Dory, snapper, groper/hapuku, gurnard, tarakihi, blue cod, monkfish, lemon fish, orange roughy and blue nose.

If I am going to heat the oven to finish the fish I will often thriftily think of something else I can cook in it as well, whether it be crispy potatoes, a pudding of some sort or bread reheated until crusty and crunchy.

Lemon and Courgette Risotto with Panfried Salmon

Like the Italians I think risotto should be kept as a dish in its own right, not used as a starch option or side dish. Here the panfried salmon is used almost as a garnish to this lemony risotto in which the rice is the star.

LEMON AND COURGETTE RISOTTO
1 large clove garlic
4 tablespoons extra virgin olive oil
1 tablespoon finely chopped young thyme leaves
grated zest of 1 large lemon
400g (14oz) vialone nano or arborio risotto rice

125ml (4fl oz) dry white wine
1/4 teaspoon toasted saffron
1 litre (1 pint 15fl oz) well-flavoured liquid chicken stock
salt and freshly ground black pepper
4 courgettes (zucchini)
juice of 1 lemon
1 tablespoon unsalted butter

SALMON
6 x 100g (31/2 oz) pieces skinned, boned salmon fillet
plain flour for dusting
4 tablespoons olive oil
lemon wedges

See also: the Basic Recipe for risotto, page 110.

Peel and finely chop the garlic. Heat the extra virgin olive oil in a deep, wide pan. Add the thyme, garlic and lemon zest and gently fry for 20 seconds. Add the rice and mix well, letting it toast for 3 minutes and become covered with oil. Add the wine and the saffron, crushed to a powder with your fingertips, and bring to the boil. Boil until the wine has evaporated. Have the chicken stock boiling and add enough boiling stock to just cover the risotto. Bring to a simmer, stirring constantly, and allow the liquid to disappear as it is absorbed into the rice as described in the Basic Recipe on page 110. Repeat until all the stock is used. Season well with salt and pepper.

Just before the final amount of stock is used, add the courgettes, sliced paper-thin lengthways, and continue cooking. Finally, stir in the lemon juice and butter.

Dust the salmon with flour and shake off the excess. Heat the olive oil in a frying pan until hot and add the salmon. Quickly fry the salmon over a high heat so that the outside browns quickly and the inside remains rare.

Remove from the pan and serve a slice of salmon on a portion of risotto with a lemon wedge for squeezing on the side.

SERVES 6

Panfried Fish with Fresh Herbs, Glass Noodles and Dipping Sauce

This is my take on a traditional Vietnamese dish that makes an excellent first course or light lunch. As with any South-east Asian inspired dish, the balance of sweet, salty, hot and sour tastes in the dipping sauce needs special attention. You can choose to balance the four flavours so that none dominates, or to let one of the flavours dominate if you prefer it that way.
Glass noodles are also called lungkow, cellophane or bean thread noodles, and are available from Asian shops.

See also:
Dipping Sauce, page 64; and the Basic Recipe for fish, page 70.

250g (9oz) glass noodles
Dipping Sauce (see recipe on
    page 64)
1 teaspoon ground turmeric
2 teaspoons fish sauce

juice of 3 limes
800g (1lb 12oz) boneless, skinless,
    firm white fish
peanut oil for frying
4 spring onions, green part only

2 handfuls dill, finely chopped
100g (3 1/2 oz) roasted unsalted
    peanuts, coarsely chopped

Cover the noodles with hot water and soak them for 25 minutes until soft and flexible. Drain and cook in boiling water for 5 minutes or until the noodles are just transparent. Drain and cool in plenty of cold water. Leave the cooked noodles in the cold water until you need them, otherwise they will stick together.

Make the dipping sauce as described on page 64, and set aside.

Mix the turmeric, fish sauce and lime juice and rub it all over the fish pieces. Set aside for 20 minutes.

Preheat the oven to 200°C (400°F). Cut the fish into 5cm (2in) pieces and fry in hot peanut oil until browned. Do this in batches so that the pan does not get crowded. Transfer the fish to an ovenproof dish and finish cooking in the oven as described in the Basic Recipe on page 70. Keep warm in the oven.

Thinly slice the spring onions. When all the fish is cooked, mix the dill and spring onions and carefully toss the fish pieces in this mixture.

Serve the fish on the well-drained cold noodles with the peanuts sprinkled on top and the dipping sauce in individual small bowls on the side.   **SERVES 4–6**

Panfried Fish with Fresh Herbs, Glass Noodles and Dipping Sauce

Panfried Fish with Tomatoes and Basil and Baked Potatoes

Three simple components are put together for this dish, which is almost like a grown up's version of fish and chips with tomato sauce. As with any simple food, the success of the dish relies on perfect ingredients cooked well. The fish needs to be fresh, the tomatoes need to be bright red, vine-ripened and full of flavour, and the potatoes must be of the floury variety so that they are crisp on the outside and fluffy inside.

Start cooking the baked potatoes first as they take about an hour to cook.

See also: the Basic Recipe for fish, page 70.

BAKED POTATOES
900g (2lb) floury potatoes
4 tablespoons olive oil
1 teaspoon Maldon sea salt

FISH WITH TOMATOES AND BASIL
6 large vine-ripened tomatoes, cored
1 clove garlic
4 x 200g (7oz) pieces skinned, boned firm white fish fillet

plain flour for dusting
6 tablespoons extra virgin olive oil
1 small dried red chilli, finely sliced
salt and freshly ground black pepper
8 basil leaves, ripped into small pieces

Preheat the oven to 200°C (400°F). Peel the potatoes and cut into rough 3cm (1¼ in) cubes. Put the olive oil, salt and potatoes into a wide roasting dish so that the potatoes are not crowded. Mix well so that they are coated with the olive oil. Place in the oven and forget about them for 1 hour until they are golden brown and crisp. Remove them from the oven and put into a paper towel-lined serving dish. Keep the oven on for the fish.

Peel the tomatoes by covering them with boiling water for 20 seconds, plunging them into cold water and pulling off the skins. Halve the tomatoes, remove the seeds with a teaspoon and discard them. Chop the tomatoes coarsely and reserve them. Peel and finely chop the garlic. Set aside.

Dust the fish in flour and shake off the excess. Heat 4 tablespoons of the extra virgin olive oil over a moderate heat in a frying pan. Add the fish and fry until golden brown on each side. Transfer the fish to an ovenproof serving dish and place in the oven to finish cooking as described in the Basic Recipe on page 70.

Pour the oil from the pan and wipe it out with paper towels. Put the pan on a moderate heat and add the remaining 2 tablespoons of extra virgin olive oil. When the oil is hot add the garlic and chilli and fry, without browning, for 15 seconds. Add the reserved tomatoes and fry them until they are hot. Season well with salt and pepper and stir in the fresh basil.

Remove the fish from the oven and pour the tomato mixture over the top.

Serve the fish and tomatoes with the potatoes on the side. **SERVES 4**

Panfried Fish with Tomato and Ginger Jam and Sticky Rice

Sweet, sour and hot flavours dominate this dish, which is good served with sliced cucumber and salad greens.

Traditionally, sticky rice or glutinous rice is soaked, then steamed in a special vessel. A Singaporean friend taught me the method below and it works just as well. The sticky rice is mixed with ordinary long grain white rice, which keeps it from becoming mushy.

Glutinous white rice is available from Asian shops. Jasmine rice is a fragrant Thai variety of long grain white rice available from supermarkets and Asian shops.

See also: the Basic Recipe for rice, page 110; and the Basic Recipe for fish, page 70.

TOMATO AND GINGER JAM
5 cloves garlic
1 small onion
3 tablespoons peanut oil
200g (7oz) peeled fresh ginger, sliced paper thin
1 teaspoon salt
2 small dried red chillies, thinly sliced
8 tomatoes, cored
250g (9oz) sugar
4 tablespoons cider vinegar

STICKY RICE
350g (12½ oz) glutinous white rice
50g (2oz) jasmine rice
500ml (18fl oz) water

FISH
4 x 200g (7oz) pieces skinless, boneless, firm white fish
plain flour for dusting
4 tablespoons peanut oil

Peel and thinly slice the garlic and onion. Heat the peanut oil in a saucepan. Add the ginger, garlic, onion, salt and chillies. Sauté, without browning, until the onion is soft.

Peel the tomatoes as described on page 74, and chop the flesh. Add them to the pan with the sugar and vinegar, bring to the boil and simmer until reduced by half, about 20 minutes. Cool.

Mix the two varieties of rice, wash well and drain. Put into a saucepan and add the water. Cook as described in the Basic Recipe on page 110.

Preheat the oven to 200°C (400°F). Dust the fish in flour and shake off the excess.

Heat the 4 tablespoons of peanut oil until hot in a large frying pan and add the fish. Fry until golden on each side then transfer the fish to an ovenproof dish to finish cooking in the oven as described in the Basic Recipe on page 70.

When the fish is just cooked through, serve the hot fish on the sticky rice with the Tomato and Ginger Jam on the side.

SERVES 4

Panfried Fish with Roasted Capsicum Salad

ROASTED CAPSICUM SALAD
1 small red onion
5 large red capsicums (peppers)
olive oil
2 tablespoons capers
3 tablespoons balsamic vinegar

4 tablespoons extra virgin olive oil
salt and freshly ground
    black pepper

PANFRIED FISH
plain flour for dusting

4 x 200g (7oz) pieces firm white
    boneless, skinless fish
6 slices 2cm (3/4 in) thick ciabatta,
    or any white sour dough bread
chopped flat-leafed parsley and
    black olives for garnish

See also: the Basic Recipe for fish, page 70.

Preheat the oven to 200°C (400°F). Peel and slice the onion.

Rub the capsicums all over with olive oil. Put them into a wide, shallow roasting dish and place in the oven, turning occasionally, until their skins bubble and blister all over. Remove from the oven and place in a bowl. Cover the bowl tightly and let them steam for 15 minutes. Uncover and peel the skins off the capsicums.

Core, seed and slice the capsicums thinly and put them into a bowl. Add the capers, onion, vinegar and olive oil. Season well with salt and pepper and set aside.

Dust the fish with flour and shake off the excess. Cook as described in the Basic Recipe on page 70, but omit the butter, lemon and capers stage.

Toast the bread and place it on a serving platter. Sit the pieces of fish on the toast and pile the salad on top. Garnish with chopped parsley and olives and serve hot or at room temperature.

SERVES 4–6

Escabèched Snapper Salad

Escabèche is a Spanish mix of water, vinegar and flavourings that was often heated and poured over fried fish to flavour and preserve it before the days of refrigeration. It tastes delicious.

4 tablespoons plain flour
1 teaspoon sweet Spanish paprika
4 x 200g (7oz) pieces skinned,
    boned snapper fillet
6 tablespoons olive oil
salt and freshly ground
    black pepper
3 cloves garlic

4 tablespoons wine vinegar
4 tablespoons white wine
2 tablespoons water
1 carrot
3 vine-ripened tomatoes
1/2 red capsicum (pepper)
12 green olives
1 small red onion

1 stick celery, thinly sliced
2 tablespoons capers
1 tablespoon chopped
    flat-leafed parsley
extra virgin olive oil for drizzling
lemon wedges for squeezing

See also: the Basic Recipe for fish, page 70.

Mix the flour and paprika together, dust the fish in this and shake off the excess. Heat 4 tablespoons of the olive oil in a frying pan over a moderate heat and panfry the fish as described in the Basic Recipe on page 70, but omit the lemon and caper stage. Put the fish onto a wide, shallow platter and season well with salt and pepper.

Wipe the pan with paper towels and add the remaining 2 tablespoons of olive oil. Peel and thinly slice the garlic, and gently fry until golden. Carefully add the vinegar, wine and water and mix well. Pour the hot mixture over the fish. Let it cool if desired or continue with the fish warm.

Peel the carrot and cut into thin strips. Core the tomatoes and cut into thin wedges. Core, seed and thinly slice the capsicum. Peel and thinly slice the onion.

Pile the carrot, tomatoes, capsicum, olives, onion and celery on top of the fish. Sprinkle the capers and parsley on top and dribble a little extra virgin olive oil over everything. Garnish with lemon wedges. Serve with crusty bread.   **SERVES 4**

Restorative comfort food

Vegetable Soup

Soup is such a restorative comfort food.
It's a great start to the meal or it can be
the meal itself, and it's the perfect vehicle
for other delicacies.

Curry Spiced Tomato and Rice Soup
Creamed Mussel and Spinach Soup
Roasted Red Onion and Potato Soup
    with Parmesan Croûtons
Chunky Italian-style Vegetable Soup
    with Tubular Pasta
Pumpkin Soup with Panfried Fish and
    Coriander Oil

Basic Recipe

'French' Vegetable Soup

2 medium-sized floury potatoes
300g (10½ oz) peeled and seeded
   pumpkin
3 cloves garlic

1 onion
1 small carrot
3 tablespoons olive oil
1 stick celery, thinly sliced
water

2 tablespoons butter
salt and freshly ground
   black pepper

Peel and dice the potatoes. Dice the pumpkin. Peel and finely chop the garlic. Peel and chop the onion and carrot.

Heat the olive oil in a saucepan over a moderate heat and add the garlic, onion, carrot and celery. Fry gently, without browning, until the onion is soft. Add the potatoes and pumpkin, cover with water and bring to the boil.

Simmer until the vegetables are soft. Remove from the heat and add the butter. Purée until smooth in a food processor, put back into a clean saucepan and bring to the boil. Taste and season well with salt and pepper.

Serve with crusty bread and freshly grated gruyère or parmesan cheese, if desired.

SERVES 4–6

The Rules

It is distressing to see people loading packet and canned soups into their shopping trolleys at the supermarket. For the same price as they pay for these so-called convenience foods they could quite easily make a simple vegetable purée, grate some cheese on top, enjoy it with a slice of crusty bread, and feel a lot better for it.

I use the simple method the French have perfected for making soup. Flavourings are slowly fried without browning, similar to making a sofrito for a stew, and then liquid, vegetables and stock, or more often simply water, are added, the vegetables are simmered until soft then puréed and the soup is enriched with butter. Freshly grated cheese is optional. While it may sound like deluxe baby food, this is a dish that always pleases.

The basic method is one that can be varied with other ingredients and puréed or not.

Curry Spiced Tomato and Rice Soup

5 cloves garlic

1 onion

3 tablespoons peanut oil

3 tablespoons finely chopped
   fresh ginger

1 small cinnamon stick

1 teaspoon ground turmeric

2 small dried red chillies (or to
   taste), finely sliced

1 teaspoon sugar

400g (14oz) Italian tomatoes
   in juice

125ml (4fl oz) water

400ml (14fl oz) canned
   coconut cream

300g (10 1/2 oz) leftover
   long grain white rice

3 tablespoons fresh lime juice

salt

coriander leaves for garnish

Peel and finely chop the garlic and onion. Heat the peanut oil over a moderate heat in a saucepan. Add the garlic, onion, ginger, cinnamon, turmeric, chillies and sugar. Sauté, without browning, until the onion is completely soft.

Purée the tomatoes in a food processor or mash them well. Add the tomatoes, water, coconut cream and rice and bring to the boil. Add the lime juice, taste, and season with the salt. Simmer, uncovered, for 4 minutes.

Serve the soup garnished with coriander.

SERVES 4

Creamed Mussel and Spinach Soup

This is one of the best mussel soups I know. Don't add salt as the mussel cooking liquid is salty.

20 medium-sized mussels

2 cloves garlic

1 large sprig parsley

125ml (4fl oz) dry white wine

1 small onion

2 small potatoes

2 tablespoons olive oil

1/4 teaspoon freshly ground
   black pepper

125ml (4fl oz) water

500ml (18fl oz) well-flavoured liquid
   chicken stock

300g (10 1/2 oz) spinach leaves

grated zest of 1 lemon

150ml (5fl oz) cream

Clean the mussels as described in The Rules on page 10. Peel and finely chop the garlic.

Put the mussels, parsley, garlic and wine into a saucepan and steam the mussels open as described in the Basic Recipe on page 10. Remove the shells and discard them as soon as the mussels are cool enough to handle. Put the mussels to one side. Strain the cooking liquid and reserve.

Peel and finely chop the onion. Peel and chop the potatoes into 2cm (3/4 in) cubes. Heat the olive oil in a saucepan and add the onion and pepper and gently fry, without browning, until the onion is soft. Add the potatoes, water, stock and the reserved mussel cooking liquid and bring to the boil. Simmer until the potatoes are soft.

Add the spinach leaves and lemon zest and bring back to the boil. Simmer for 4 minutes. Remove from the heat and pour into a food processor or blender, add the cooked mussels and process until smooth.

Return to a clean saucepan and stir in the cream. Bring the soup to the boil and serve with crusty bread.

SERVES 4–6

See also: The Rules for mussels, page 10; and the Basic Recipe for mussels, page 10.

Roasted Red Onion and Potato Soup with Parmesan Croûtons

Roasting some of the vegetables first gives the soup a smoky, caramelised taste and means the initial gentle frying stage is unnecessary. The pink colour of the onions is stunning.

PARMESAN CROÛTONS

4 tablespoons olive oil

1/2 French loaf, cut into 2cm (3/4 in) cubes

150g (5oz) fresh, finely grated parmesan cheese

4 tablespoons finely chopped flat-leafed parsley

SOUP

3 medium-sized red onions

2 cloves garlic

juice of 1/2 lemon

2 tablespoons olive oil

salt and freshly ground black pepper

700g (1lb 9oz) floury potatoes

1 litre (1 pint 15fl oz) well-flavoured liquid chicken stock

2 tablespoons chopped flat-leafed parsley

Heat the olive oil in a large frying pan until hot but not smoking. Add the bread and fry, stirring continuously, until the bread cubes are uniformly golden brown.

Remove from the pan and put into a large bowl. Add the parmesan cheese and parsley and toss well so that everything is evenly distributed. Set aside to cool.

Peel and thinly slice the onions. Peel and finely chop the garlic. Preheat the oven to 200°C (400°F). Put the onions, lemon juice, 2 tablespoons of olive oil and garlic into a wide, shallow roasting tray. Season well with salt and pepper and place in the oven for 25 minutes until soft and beginning to brown.

Peel and chop the potatoes. Put the potatoes and stock into a saucepan and bring to the boil. Simmer until the potatoes are soft. Add the roasted onions and simmer for 2 minutes, then remove from the heat and purée in a food processor until smooth. Add the parsley, mix well, taste and season again.

Serve sprinkled with plenty of parmesan cheese croûtons.

SERVES 4–6

Chunky Italian-style Vegetable Soup with Tubular Pasta

A meal in a plate, this thick, stew-like vegetable soup is served here with pasta.

SOUP
3 rashers rindless bacon
1 red capsicum (pepper)
250g (9oz) peeled and seeded
   pumpkin
3 large cloves garlic
1 onion
1 small carrot
3 tablespoons olive oil
1 stick celery, thinly sliced

2 courgettes (zucchini), sliced
1 sprig fresh rosemary
700g (1lb 9oz) tomatoes, or 400g
   (14oz) can Italian tomatoes in
   juice, mashed
2 tablespoons tomato paste
500ml (18fl oz) well-flavoured
   liquid chicken stock
500ml (18fl oz) water
2 tablespoons parsley

salt and freshly ground
   black pepper
freshly grated parmesan cheese
   for sprinkling

PASTA
300g (10½ oz) short tubular pasta
   (rigatoni or penne rigate
   are suitable)

See also: the Basic Recipe for pasta, page 122.

Slice the bacon into thin strips. Core, seed and dice the capsicum. Cut the pumpkin into 2cm (1in) cubes. Peel and finely chop the garlic. Peel and chop the onion and carrot.

Heat the olive oil in a large saucepan over a moderate heat. Add the bacon, capsicum, pumpkin, garlic, onion, carrot, celery, courgettes, and rosemary. Fry gently, without browning, until the onion is soft.

If using fresh tomatoes, peel and chop them. Add the tomatoes, tomato paste, stock and water and bring to the boil. Mix well and simmer for 30 minutes until the vegetables are very tender. Season with salt and pepper to taste.

Cook the pasta as described in the Basic Recipe on page 122.

Serve the vegetable soup over some of the pasta with freshly grated parmesan cheese sprinkled on top.

SERVES 6

Pumpkin Soup with Panfried Fish and Coriander Oil

Soup turned into a main course. The three components, soup, fried fish and highly flavoured coriander and garlic oil, make a stunning main course. The soup and oil can be prepared in advance. All that is needed is a green salad to follow.
Snapper, John Dory, gurnard, hapuku, groper or bluenose are all suitable fish to use.

CORIANDER OIL
1 clove garlic
100ml (3$\frac{1}{2}$ fl oz) olive oil
1 large handful coriander leaves
   and stalks
pinch of salt

PUMPKIN SOUP
3 cloves garlic
1 small onion

900g (2lb) peeled and seeded
   pumpkin
4 tablespoons olive oil
2 small dried red chillies,
   finely sliced
1 litre (1 pint 15fl oz) well-flavoured
   liquid chicken stock
1 teaspoon sugar
salt and freshly ground
   black pepper

FISH
4 x 150g (5oz) pieces skinned,
   boned firm white fish
plain flour for dusting

4 x 2cm (3/4 in) thick slices ciabatta
   or other sourdough bread

See also: *the Basic Recipe for fish, page 70.*

Peel and chop the garlic for the coriander oil. Put the garlic, olive oil, coriander leaves and salt into a food processor or blender and process until smooth. Set aside.

Peel and finely chop the garlic and onion for the soup. Dice the pumpkin. Heat 4 tablespoons of olive oil over a moderate heat in a saucepan and add the garlic, onion and chillies. Fry gently, without browning, until the onion is soft.

   Add the pumpkin, stock and sugar and bring to the boil. Simmer gently until the pumpkin is soft.

   Remove from the heat, purée until smooth in a food processor, return to a clean saucepan, taste and season with salt and pepper and bring to the boil.

Dust the fish with flour and shake off any excess. Panfry as described in the Basic Recipe on page 70, but omit the capers and lemon stage.

Toast the bread. Serve a piece of fish on a piece of toast on the bottom of a wide soup plate with the soup poured around it and the coriander oil dribbled on top.   **SERVES 4**

Roasted

Vegetables

Thinly sliced vegetables, perfumed with olive oil, garlic and freshly ground black pepper and quickly caramelised in a hot oven. People love vegetables cooked this way, and they are wonderfully easy to prepare.

Panfried Salmon with Warm Roasted
   Tomato Vinaigrette and Rocket
Panfried Steak with Balsamic Vinegar
   and Roasted Asparagus
Indian Spiced Potatoes with
   Panfried Fish and Minted Yoghurt
Roasted Carrot and Orange Salad
Roasted Pumpkin and Red
   Capsicum Soup

Roasted Seasonal Vegetables

Once you have roasted vegetables like this a few times you will soon recognise by their appearance and aroma when they are ready. It is important to watch them and not to undercook or overcook them.

4 cloves garlic
3 medium-sized red onions, unpeeled
2 red capsicums (peppers)
1 yellow capsicum (pepper)

100g (3½ oz) green beans
2 courgettes (zucchini)
1 carrot
1 parsnip
1 small eggplant (aubergine)

10 cherry tomatoes
50ml (2fl oz) extra virgin olive oil, plus extra
Maldon sea salt and freshly ground black pepper

Peel and finely chop the garlic, quarter the onions, core, seed and quarter the capsicums, cut the stalk ends off the beans. Trim the ends off the courgettes and cut them lengthways into ½ cm (⅛ in) thick slices. Peel the carrot and parsnip and cut them lengthways into ½ cm (¼ in) thick slices. Cut the eggplant into 1cm (½ in) thick slices. Preheat the oven to 200°C (400°F).

Put the vegetables onto a large shallow baking tray, don't crowd them, and use 2 trays if necessary. Add the extra virgin olive oil and garlic and season well with salt and pepper. Toss everything so that the oil and the flavourings are evenly distributed.

Place in the oven and roast for 20 minutes, giving the vegetables an occasional toss, until they are browned, slightly shrivelled, the parsnip is cooked through and everything else is cooked but firm to the bite.

Remove from the oven and eat as is, or as an accompaniment to a roast chicken, fried fish, panfried steak or on pasta with plenty of freshly grated parmesan cheese. **SERVES 4–6**

Basic Recipe

The Rules

Remember the huge popularity among restaurant chefs in the early 1990s for chargrilling absolutely everything? Starting in California and emanating in ripples like an atomic explosion across the affluent world, chefs and diners were hemmed in by sheets of flame as more and more food hit the chargrill. The one thing that did benefit from the chargrill revolution was vegetable cookery. Chargrilled vegetables are delicious. Roasted vegetables produce almost the same results.

The principle behind vegetables roasted in this way is simple. You need to make sure that any mixture of vegetables will cook quickly at the same time, so cut and slice them into similar thicknesses.

Make sure root vegetables and tubers are completely cooked, and everything else, while being browned and slightly shrivelled, is cooked 'al dente', or firm to the bite. Roasted vegetables are good hot or cold, as finger food with drinks, as a salad with dressing, or as an accompaniment to the main course, and they don't need to be flavoured with much else apart from olive oil, garlic, pepper and salt, although there are lots of excellent flavours you can choose to add to them.

From an aesthetic point of view, vegetables roasted like this look better when their natural shape is still recognisable, so don't chop them up too small. It is better just to make sure they are in thin slices with as many different shapes and colours as possible. One thing worth remembering is that vegetables cooked like this shrink, so always cook a few more than you think you'll need.

Panfried Salmon with Warm Roasted Tomato Vinaigrette and Rocket

The fragrance of these roasting, smoked paprika-dusted tomatoes is intoxicating. Tomatoes have a natural acidity that can vary according to the tomatoes used, so taste the vinaigrette and then decide if it needs more or less vinegar. It should not be mouth-puckeringly sour.

See also: the Basic Recipe for fish, page 70.

ROASTED TOMATO VINAIGRETTE
2 cloves garlic
5 vine-ripened tomatoes
6 tablespoons extra virgin olive oil
1 teaspoon sweet Spanish paprika

salt and freshly ground
  black pepper
1 tablespoon sherry vinegar
  or to taste
2 teaspoons sugar

SALMON
4 x 150g (5oz) pieces skinned,
  boned salmon fillet
plain flour for dusting
4 tablespoons olive oil
2 handfuls rocket leaves

Preheat the oven to 200°C (400°F). Peel and finely chop the garlic. Core the tomatoes, cut a small cross shape in the skin on top of each and put the tomatoes into a small roasting dish. Pour 4 tablespoons of the extra virgin olive oil over them and sprinkle the garlic and paprika on top. Season well with salt and pepper.

Roast in the oven until the tomatoes are well browned and sizzling but not collapsing, about 15–20 minutes. Remove from the oven. Put the tomatoes into a bowl and add the remaining 2 tablespoons of olive oil, vinegar to taste, and the sugar. Mix gently, taste and season again with salt and pepper. Set aside.

Dust the salmon with flour and shake off the excess. Heat the olive oil over a moderate heat, panfry the salmon as described in the Basic Recipe on page 70, and finish cooking it in the oven. Omit the lemon and capers.

Serve the salmon on a serving platter with rocket leaves on the side and the vinaigrette spooned over the top.

SERVES 4

Panfried Steak with Balsamic Vinegar and Roasted Asparagus

Have the asparagus ready when the steak is ready.
The steak weight is the trimmed weight, after all the fat and sinew has been removed.

See also: The Rules for steak, page 59.

ASPARAGUS
1 clove garlic
350g (12¹/₂ oz) asparagus
4 tablespoons olive oil
salt and freshly ground
    black pepper

STEAK
2 cloves garlic
4 x 150g (5oz) pieces eye fillet steak
4 tablespoons olive oil
50ml (2fl oz) well-flavoured liquid
    beef stock

50ml (2fl oz) balsamic vinegar
2 tablespoons butter

Preheat the oven to 200°C (400°F). Peel and finely chop the clove of garlic. Snap the bottom ends off the asparagus, put the asparagus onto a flat oven tray and pour the olive oil over it. Sprinkle the chopped garlic over and season well with salt and pepper. Toss everything so that everything is evenly distributed.

Roast in the oven for 10 minutes, or until the asparagus is slightly shrivelled, just beginning to brown but still firm to the bite. Bite the end off a spear to see if it is ready. Remove the asparagus from the oven.

Peel and crush to a paste the 2 cloves of garlic. Rub the garlic paste all over the pieces of steak.

Heat the olive oil until hot but not smoking. Panfry the steak over a moderately high heat until cooked to your liking. Use the touch test as described in the The Rules on page 59 to tell if it is ready.

Transfer the pieces of steak to a warm plate and keep them warm. Pour the fat out of the pan and add the beef stock and vinegar. Bring to the boil and boil until the mixture starts to look syrupy. Stir in the butter and remove from the heat. Put each piece of steak on a warm plate with some of the asparagus. Spoon a little of the balsamic vinegar sauce over the steak and serve it immediately. Good with Potato Gratin (see page 49). **SERVES 4**

Indian Spiced Potatoes with Panfried Fish and Minted Yoghurt

This is a bit like an Indian version of fish and chips. Potatoes are the vegetable that takes the longest to roast. A little water is added to the mixture to help distribute the spices over the potatoes and to prevent the spices burning before the potatoes are cooked.
The minted yoghurt is like a classic Indian raita, which is the cooling yoghurt relish served at most Indian meals.

MINTED YOGHURT
1/2 peeled cucumber
250ml (9fl oz) plain
   unsweetened yoghurt
1 handful mint leaves,
   thinly sliced
salt

SPICED POTATOES
1 kg (2lb 3oz) floury potatoes
5 cloves garlic
1 teaspoon salt
1 teaspoon ground turmeric
2 teaspoons cumin seeds
1 teaspoon yellow mustard seeds
2 small dried red chillies,
   finely sliced

juice of 1 lemon
100ml (3 1/2 fl oz) water
4 tablespoons peanut oil

FISH
4 x 200g (7oz) pieces skinned,
   boned firm white fish fillets
plain flour for dusting

See also: the Basic Recipe for fish, page 70.

Grate the cucumber and squeeze it dry. Mix the cucumber, yoghurt and mint together well. Season to taste with salt. Set aside.

Preheat the oven to 200°C (400°F). Peel the potatoes and cut into large, bite-sized chunks. Peel and finely chop the garlic. Put the potatoes, salt, garlic, turmeric, cumin seeds, mustard seeds, chillies, lemon juice, water and peanut oil into a roasting dish just big enough to hold them and mix well.

Place in the oven and roast for 1 hour, turn everything over and gently mix frequently. The water will evaporate and by the time the potatoes are cooked they will have crisped. When serving scrape all the crunchy toasted spices out of the bottom of the pan as these are delicious.

Dust the fish with flour and shake off the excess. Panfry as described in the Basic Recipe on page 70, but omit the capers and lemon.

Serve the fish with some of the potatoes beside it and the minted yoghurt on the side for everyone to help themselves.   **SERVES 4**

Roasted Carrot and Orange Salad

This salad has a dazzling colour and subtle Middle Eastern tastes. It makes a good meze, the Greek name for an appetiser to go with drinks (just serve it on some good bread), as well as being excellent with simply fried fish or roast chicken or lamb.

8 medium-sized carrots
1 teaspoon cumin seeds
2 oranges
grated zest of 1 orange

50ml (2fl oz) extra virgin olive oil
salt and freshly ground black pepper
juice of 1 lemon

10 mint leaves ripped into small pieces

Preheat the oven to 200°C (400°F). Peel the carrots, remove the ends and slice the carrots very thinly lengthways into ribbons. Toast the cumin seeds in a dry pan until they are just beginning to darken and you can smell their fragrance. Peel the oranges with a sharp knife and cut the flesh into 1/2 cm (1/4 in) rounds.

Put the carrot ribbons onto a large shallow oven tray (use two trays if they look crowded). Add the orange zest, cumin seeds and extra virgin olive oil and season well with salt and pepper. Toss everything well and place in the oven for 20 minutes, or until they are browned and starting to shrivel. Give the carrot ribbons a toss while they roast.

Remove from the oven and put them into a shallow salad bowl. Add the sliced oranges and lemon juice and mix gently. Sprinkle the mint leaves on top and serve.

SERVES 4–6

Roasted Pumpkin and Red Capsicum Soup

Roasting the vegetables first gives a delicious taste to a simple vegetable soup.

700g (1lb 9oz) pumpkin
1 red capsicum (pepper)
4 tablespoons olive oil
6 whole cloves garlic, peeled

2 small dried red chillies, finely sliced
salt and freshly ground black pepper

1 litre (1 pint 15fl oz) well-flavoured liquid chicken stock
1 ripe Hass avocado
fresh coriander leaves

Preheat the oven to 200°C (400°F). Cut the pumpkin into 1cm (1/2 in) thick slices. Core, seed and quarter the capsicum. Put the olive oil, pumpkin, capsicum, garlic and chillies into a large, shallow roasting tray and mix well so that the oil coats everything. Season well with salt and pepper.

Place in the oven and roast for 45 minutes until the pumpkin is tender. Remove from the oven. Put the chicken stock into a saucepan and add the vegetables from the roasting tray. Bring to the boil.

Remove from the heat and purée in a food processor. Taste and season again with salt and pepper. Return to a clean saucepan and bring to the boil.

Peel, stone and slice the avocado. Serve the soup garnished with avocado slices and coriander leaves.

SERVES 4–6

Roasted Carrot and Orange Salad

Slowly, slowly, slowly

Stew

Stews of one form or another can be found in most cuisines. They range in taste and appearance from spicy, vividly coloured Indian curries to aromatic French daubes.

Chicken Drumsticks with Red Onion, Potato and Rocket Sofrito and Pumpkin Seed Vinaigrette

Tomato Sofrito and Mussels with Pasta

Mussel, Fish and Chorizo Stew

Mediterranean Vegetable Stew with Spicy Couscous

Kumara, Pumpkin and Spinach Curry with Coconut Rice

French Lamb and Spring Vegetable Stew on 'Green' Rice

Beef Stewed in Red Wine

2 cloves garlic

2 onions

1 carrot

4 tablespoons olive oil

1.5kg (3lb 5oz) lean, cross-cut
    blade steak, cut into 4cm
    (1½ in) cubes

1 stick celery, thinly sliced

4cm (1½ in) long piece orange
    peel, no pith

1 cinnamon stick

2 fresh bay leaves

2 tablespoons chopped
    flat-leafed parsley

1½ tablespoons plain flour

1 tablespoon tomato paste

salt and freshly ground
    black pepper

500ml (18fl oz) red wine

500ml (18fl oz) well-flavoured
    liquid beef stock

Preheat the oven to 180°C (350°F). Peel and finely chop the garlic. Peel and chop the onions. Peel and thinly slice the carrot.

Heat the olive oil until hot but not smoking in a heavy metal casserole and add the meat. Brown the meat all over and transfer to a plate.

Lower the heat to moderate and add the garlic, onions, carrot, celery, orange peel, cinnamon stick, bay leaves and parsley. Gently

fry, without browning, until the onion is soft (don't worry about the carrot) as described in The Rules opposite.

Add the meat and any juices to the casserole, sprinkle the flour over and add the tomato paste. Season well with salt and pepper. Mix well.

Add the wine and stock and mix well. Bring to the boil, cover and place in the oven. Cook for 2 hours or until the meat is very tender and the sauce slightly thickened. Remove from the oven and let the stew rest for 5 minutes. Uncover and stir carefully.

Serve with mashed floury potatoes and a salad to follow.   **SERVES 4–6**

'Stew' is not a word that is considered attractive these days but all dishes that are made by slowly frying vegetables, herbs and spices with meat, fish, vegetables or pulses, and then adding liquid, be it water, stock or wine, and simmering the mixture until thickened and well cooked, can be classed as 'stews'.

The first operation when making a stew is the slow frying of the herbs or spices and vegetables. Onions, either alone or with other vegetables, are universally used in this stage. In Spain the initial frying is called a 'sofrito', which is the term I use. Sofrito is one of the most basic and most important parts of my cooking repertoire. A sofrito, as well as being part of a stew, is also a dish in its own right.

To make a successful sofrito that has the concentrated flavour of the vegetables, herbs and spices needed to be a dish by itself, or be strong enough to flavour a stew, you must allow enough time for the sofrito to slowly fry without browning. This slow cooking is the only way to avoid a sour taste and raw texture. Onions will not soften and become sweet and aromatic by being cooked in liquid; they need initial softening in oil.

The slower onions are fried, the better they will taste. This process needs all of your senses to be successful. Listen for the sound of them softly frying – anything above a sighing sound means the pan is too hot. The smell of the onions should be sweetly aromatic, not with any burning smell. The look of the onions when ready is crucial; they should look as if they have melted and be transparently golden. When you taste them they should feel completely melt-in-the-mouth soft to the bite and taste sweet and mild. Any combination of sofrito ingredients should perform the same way.

Meat, vegetables, fish or pulses are added next, and liquid to stew them in. The mixture is then carefully cooked by either being simmered on top of the stove or in the oven. This cooking is slow so that the meat, vegetable or pulses are made tender and the liquid evaporates enough to thicken slightly.

If meat is used, the stew needs to be set aside after it is cooked, off the heat, to rest while the meat reabsorbs the liquid so that it will not be dry.

Long cooking is important – it ensures well-developed flavours, a characteristic everyone appreciates.

The Rules

Chicken Drumsticks with Red Onion, Potato and Rocket Sofrito, and Pumpkin Seed Vinaigrette

This recipe shows how a sofrito can become the main part of a meal.

CHICKEN DRUMSTICKS
8 chicken drumsticks,
    bone ends cut off
2 tablespoons brown sugar
3 tablespoons sherry vinegar
1 teaspoon salt
2 tablespoons olive oil

SOFRITO
4 waxy potatoes
6 medium-sized red onions
1 small carrot
4 cloves garlic
3 tablespoons extra virgin olive oil
grated zest and juice of 1 lemon
1 large sprig fresh thyme
1 handful rocket leaves
salt and freshly ground
    black pepper

PUMPKIN SEED VINAIGRETTE
75g (3oz) pumpkin seeds
1 clove garlic
125ml (4fl oz) extra virgin olive oil
juice of 1 large lemon
salt

See also: The Rules for stew, page 99.

Preheat the oven to 190°C (375°F). Put the chicken drumsticks, brown sugar, vinegar, salt and olive oil into a roasting dish and mix well. Roast for 30 minutes until the chicken is well browned and cooked through. Keep warm.

Peel the potatoes and cut into 2cm (3/4 in) cubes. Peel and slice the onions. Peel the carrot and cut into 1cm (1/2 in) cubes. Peel and finely chop the garlic.

Heat the 3 tablespoons extra virgin olive oil in a large, deep frying pan over a low heat. Add the onions, potatoes, carrot, lemon zest and juice, garlic and thyme and mix well. Gently fry, without browning, for 30 minutes or until the onions are very soft and the potatoes are tender as described in The Rules on page 99. Discard the thyme, slice the rocket thinly and stir it through the mixture so that it wilts. Season with salt and freshly ground black pepper to taste.

Toast the pumpkin seeds in a dry pan until they pop. Peel and chop the clove of garlic. Put the pumpkin seeds, 125ml extra virgin olive oil, lemon juice and garlic into a food processor and purée until smooth. Season with salt to taste.

Serve the drumsticks on the sofrito with the vinaigrette dribbled over the top.

SERVES 4

Chicken Drumsticks with Red Onion, Potato and Rocket Sofrito, and Pumpkin Seed Vinaigrette

Tomato Sofrito and Mussels with Pasta

Here the mussels are steamed open on an aromatic sofrito of onions and tomatoes.

4 tablespoons olive oil
3 cloves garlic
2 onions
6 large vine-ripened tomatoes
12 black olives

freshly ground black pepper
24 small mussels
2 tablespoons finely chopped
    flat-leafed parsley

enough cooked pasta for four
    people, tossed in a little
    extra virgin olive oil

See also: The Rules for mussels, page 10; and the Basic Recipe for pasta, page 122.

Heat the olive oil over a moderate heat in a deep frying pan. Peel and finely chop the garlic and onions and add them to the pan. Gently fry until the onions are soft. Core and halve the tomatoes and add with the olives and a good grind of pepper. Increase the heat until the tomatoes start to cook down and collapse. Mix well.

Using a pair of tongs, pull the skins off the tomatoes and discard them. If the skins won't come off, cook the tomatoes a little longer until the skins loosen.

Clean the mussels as described in The Rules on page 10. Add the mussels and parsley to the sofrito and mix well. Transfer the mussels to a warm serving dish as they open.

Time the pasta so that it is ready with the sofrito. Cook as described in the Basic Recipe on page 122.

Mix the sofrito sauce and pour it over the mussels. Serve the mussels and sauce on the hot pasta.

SERVES 4

Mussel, Fish and Chorizo Stew

Spicy chorizo sausages go well with seafood. Any firm white fish can be used.

1/2 teaspoon saffron
2 cloves garlic
1 onion
1 small carrot
3 tablespoons olive oil
12 mussels

400g (14oz) skinned, boned firm
    white fish
1 chorizo sausage, thinly sliced
125ml (4fl oz) white wine
250ml (9fl oz) well-flavoured liquid
    chicken or fish stock

75g (3oz) peas
75g (3oz) whole kernel corn
2 tablespoons finely chopped
    flat-leafed parsley

See also: the Basic Recipe for stew, page 98; The Rules and Basic Recipe for mussels, page 10; and the Basic Recipe for rice, page 110.

Carefully toast the saffron in a dry pan. Remove from the heat and put it on a plate to cool. Crush the saffron to a powder with your fingers. Peel and finely chop the garlic, onion and carrot.

Heat the olive oil over a moderate heat in a deep frying pan. Add the garlic, saffron, onion and carrot and gently fry, without browning, until the onion is soft as described in the Basic Recipe on page 98. This is the sofrito.

Clean the mussels as described in The Rules on page 10. Cut the fish into 3cm (1in)

pieces. Add the sausage, mussels, fish, wine, stock, peas and corn, and bring to the boil. Simmer until the mussels are open as described in the Basic Recipe on page 10, and the fish is cooked. Stir in the parsley. Taste; it will not need seasoning as the mussels are salty and the chorizo peppery.

Serve the stew on steamed white rice, cooked as described in the Basic Recipe on page 110.

SERVES 4

Mediterranean Vegetable Stew with Spicy Couscous

These two separate sofritos go together to make a great meal. The stew makes a good accompaniment to roast lamb or braised lamb shanks.

VEGETABLE STEW
3 cloves garlic
1 onion
1 carrot
3 tablespoons olive oil
1 large sprig fresh thyme
2 tablespoons finely chopped
    flat-leafed parsley
1 stick celery, sliced
1 teaspoon salt
1/2 teaspoon freshly ground
    black pepper
1 red capsicum (pepper)

1 small eggplant (aubergine)
300g (10 1/2 oz) can chickpeas
3 courgettes (zucchini),
    sliced thickly
12 black olives
400g (14oz) can Italian tomatoes
    in juice, mashed
2 tablespoons tomato paste
250ml (9fl oz) water

COUSCOUS
3 cloves garlic
1 onion

3 tablespoons olive oil
2 tablespoons finely chopped
    fresh ginger
1 tablespoon sweet Spanish
    smoked paprika
2 small dried red chillies,
    finely chopped
2 tablespoons chopped coriander
1 teaspoon salt
250g (9oz) instant couscous
boiling water

See also: *The Rules for stew, page 99.*

Peel and finely chop the garlic. Peel and chop the onion and carrot. Heat the olive oil over a moderate heat and add the garlic, thyme, parsley, onion, carrot, celery, salt and pepper. Gently fry until the onion is soft, as described in The Rules on page 99.

Core, seed and slice the capsicum. Cut the eggplant into 3cm (1 1/4 in) cubes. Wash and drain the chickpeas well. Add the capsicum, eggplant, courgettes, chickpeas and olives. Mix well and fry, without browning, for 3 minutes.

Add the tomatoes, tomato paste and water and bring to the boil. Simmer until the vegetables are all tender and the sauce is thick, 20–30 minutes.

Peel and finely chop the 3 cloves of garlic and the onion. Heat the olive oil for the couscous over a moderate heat in a small frying pan. Add the garlic, ginger, paprika, chillies, coriander, onion and salt, and gently fry until the onion is soft, as described in The Rules on page 99.

Put the couscous into a large, heatproof bowl. Add the onion and spice mixture and mix well. Pour in enough boiling water to cover, mix well, cover tightly with tinfoil, and set aside for 25 minutes.

Uncover and fluff up with a fork. It will still be hot. Serve the vegetable stew on the couscous. This tastes good with a dollop of plain unsweetened yoghurt.

SERVES 4–6

Kumara, Pumpkin and Spinach Curry with Coconut Rice

This vegetable curry is a kind of stew, served here with steamed rice that has been flavoured with an onion, cinnamon and coconut sofrito.

See also: The Rules for stew, page 99.

CURRY

2 medium-sized kumara (sweet potatoes)
400g (14oz) peeled and seeded pumpkin
2 onions
4 cloves garlic
4 tablespoons peanut oil
3 tablespoons peeled, finely chopped fresh ginger
2 small dried red chillies, thinly sliced
1 tablespoon toasted cumin seeds
1 teaspoon ground turmeric
1 teaspoon salt
1/2 teaspoon cracked black pepper
water
1 handful spinach leaves
125ml (4fl oz) plain unsweetened yoghurt

COCONUT RICE

400g (14oz) long grain white rice
1 onion
3 tablespoons peanut oil
1 cinnamon stick
100g (3 1/2 oz) long thread desiccated coconut
grated zest of 1 lime
1 teaspoon salt
600ml (21fl oz) water

Peel the kumara and cut into 4cm (1 1/2 in) cubes. Cut the pumpkin into 4cm (1 1/2 in) cubes. Peel and chop the onions. Peel and finely chop the garlic.

Heat the 4 tablespoons of peanut oil over a moderate heat in a deep frying pan or wide saucepan. Add the onions, ginger, garlic, chillies, cumin seeds, turmeric, salt and pepper. Gently fry, without browning, until the onion is soft, as described in The Rules on page 99.

Add the kumara and pumpkin and add enough water to just cover. Mix well. Bring to the boil and simmer until the vegetables are tender, the water partially evaporated and the mixture thick. Stir in the spinach and let it wilt. Remove from the heat and gently stir in the yoghurt.

Wash and drain the rice well. Peel and finely chop the onion for the rice. Heat the 3 tablespoons of peanut oil over a moderate heat and add the onion, cinnamon stick, three-quarters of the coconut and the lime zest. Gently fry, without browning, until the onion is soft.

Add the rice and salt and mix well. Add the water, mix well and bring to the boil. Cover tightly, turn the heat down to the lowest setting, and cook for 20 minutes without uncovering for any reason.

Toast the remaining quarter of the coconut in a dry pan until browned.

Remove the rice from the heat and let it stand, without uncovering, for 5 minutes. Uncover and fluff up with a fork.

Serve the curry on the rice and sprinkle everything with the toasted coconut.

SERVES 4–6

French Lamb and Spring Vegetable Stew on 'Green' Rice

The first cookbook I ever bought when I was a student was Elizabeth David's French Country Cooking, and the first thing I ever made for other people was the Navarin Printanier (lamb stew with spring vegetables) from that book. It was a howling success, so I have always had an affection for succulent lamb stews with vegetables! Here is my version, with a nod to the great Ms David.

FRENCH LAMB AND SPRING VEGETABLE STEW

3 cloves garlic
2 onions
2 tablespoons olive oil
grated zest of 1 lemon
1 large sprig rosemary
2 fresh bay leaves
600g (1lb 5oz) lean lamb leg
    or shoulder, cut into
    2cm (3/4 in) cubes
2 tablespoons plain flour
1/2 teaspoon salt
1/2 teaspoon freshly ground black
    pepper
250ml (9fl oz) dry white wine
500ml (18fl oz) well-flavoured
    liquid beef stock
400ml (14fl oz) water
12 baby carrots
12 button mushrooms
8 spears of asparagus
75g (3oz) fresh or frozen peas

'GREEN' RICE

400g (14oz) well washed and
    drained long grain white rice
500ml (18fl oz) water
2 tablespoons butter
1 small clove garlic
4 tablespoons each of finely
    chopped chives, flat-leafed
    parsley and chervil
finely grated zest of 1 lemon
salt and freshly ground
    black pepper

See also: the Basic Recipe for rice, page 110.

Peel and finely chop the garlic and onions. Heat the olive oil in a wide, deep pan over a moderate heat. Add the garlic, onions, lemon zest, rosemary and bay leaves. Gently fry until the onions are soft and lightly browned. Add the lamb, mix well, and fry until the lamb has coloured all over.

Add the flour, salt and pepper and mix well. Add the wine, stock and water and bring to the boil, stirring continuously. Add the carrots and mushrooms and mix well. Simmer for 45 minutes until the lamb is very tender.

Snap the bottom ends off the asparagus and cut each spear in half. Add the asparagus and peas and simmer for a further 5 minutes.

Remove from the heat and let it stand for 5 minutes to allow the meat to absorb the sauce.

Cook the rice in the water as described in the Basic Recipe on page 110. Remove from the heat and let it stand for 5 minutes. Uncover, add the butter and fluff up with a fork. Peel and finely chop the garlic. Stir in the herbs, garlic and lemon zest and season well with salt and pepper.

Serve the stew on the rice.   **SERVES 4–6**

French Lamb and Spring Vegetable Stew on 'Green' Rice

Steamed

Rice and Risotto

Essential grains

While steamed rice and risotto may be made from the same species of plant, the types of rice used for each of these dishes are very different in their cultural associations and the way they are used. Gone are the days when people thought that all rice was the same and any rice would do for any dish.

Roast Chicken Stuffed with Rice and Chinese Mushrooms
Warm Mussel and Rice Salad
Pumpkin and Almond Pilaf with Harissa
Lamb Shank Stew with Pumpkin Risotto and Gremolata
Parmesan Risotto with Roasted Vegetables
Risotto with Lemon and Fennel
Risotto with Garden Greens and Bacon

Basic Recipes

Steamed White Rice

Use this method for long grain white rice including basmati, jasmine, Australian long grain white, Japanese sushi rice, other short grain white rice (but not Italian or Spanish rices), long or short grain glutinous white rice, long or short grain brown rice (but soak it for at least 6 hours for beautifully soft rice and cook it covered for 45 minutes instead of the 20 minutes specified below).

I allow at least 100g (3¹/2 oz) raw rice per person when steaming rice. Wash the rice under running water until the water runs clear. This washes any milling starch off the grains and ensures that the rice will not be gluey. Soak the rice for at least 20 minutes to ensure tender rice and also to ensure that very long grains of rice such as basmati remain tender and do not break up when cooked.

Put the rice into a saucepan that can be covered tightly. Fill with water so that when you rest the tip of your index finger on the surface of the rice, the water comes up to the first joint of your finger. Bring to the boil. Turn the heat down to the lowest setting – the lowest gas setting is just right, but the lowest electric setting is too hot so, if using electric power, put a heat-diffusing mat under the saucepan or make a grid out of a couple of metal skewers and rest the saucepan on that.

Cover tightly and cook for exactly 20 minutes. Do not uncover during this time for any reason, otherwise the miracle of absorption will not take place. Turn off the heat and set aside for 5–10 minutes. Uncover and fluff up the rice with a fork.

This method is so successful that I do not bother cooking rice any other way, except, of course, if I am making risotto or paella.

Fresh Herb Risotto

This makes a good first course. Remember to use only arborio, vialone nano or carnaroli rice.

3 tablespoons olive oil
2 cloves garlic
1 onion
1 small carrot
1 large sprig fresh thyme
1 stick celery, finely diced

¹/2 teaspoon salt
¹/2 teaspoon freshly ground
　　black pepper
400g (14oz) Italian risotto rice
1 litre (35fl oz) well-flavoured
　　liquid chicken stock

125 ml (4fl oz) dry white wine
2 tablespoons butter
2 tablespoons chopped
　　flat-leafed parsley
2 tablespoons finely sliced chives
fresh parmesan cheese

See also: The Rules for stew, page 99.

Peel and finely chop the garlic and onion, and peel and finely dice the carrot.

Heat the olive oil over a moderate heat and add the garlic, onion, carrot, thyme, celery, salt and pepper. Gently fry, without browning, until the onion is soft, as described in The Rules on page 99. Add the rice and mix well.

'Toast' the rice, frying gently, stirring, over moderate heat for 3 minutes.

Meanwhile, bring the stock to the boil and keep it simmering. Add the wine to the rice mixture and bring to the boil. Mix well and boil until the wine evaporates. Start adding the simmering stock, about 125ml (4fl oz) at a time,

stirring continuously, over a moderate heat until you see that the rice has absorbed the stock. Continue until all the stock has been absorbed. Take your time – this process cannot be hurried, and will take at least 20 minutes.

When all the stock has been absorbed, taste some of the rice. It should be firm to the bite but tender, and the risotto should be smooth and creamy. Add the butter and mix well. Stir in the herbs, taste and correct the seasoning with salt and pepper, if necessary.

Serve immediately, sprinkled with freshly finely grated parmesan cheese.

SERVES 4–6

Steamed Rice

Basmati rice will not do for Chinese food and long grain rice is no good for sushi, so use the rice specific to the cuisine of the dish you are making. Properly steamed white rice grains should be separate, but they should stick together slightly without being stodgy or gluey. If you use the Basic Recipe you will achieve this without having to use parboiled or converted rice, which has a waxy texture and is inappropriate to almost every cuisine.

Risotto

Italian rice is of the short grain variety and is grown in the north of Italy. It is the only rice suitable for risotto, one of the great dishes of the Piedmont and Veneto areas. Three main varieties are grown: arborio, which is the cheapest; vialone nano, a firm-centred rice that is a favourite with cooks as it can be part cooked and finished later; and carnaroli, which has a very firm centre and is the hardest to overcook. I always use vialone nano or carnaroli rices whenever possible. Risotto rice is never washed before use, as washing would remove the starch from the outside of the grains and make the risotto less creamy.

The traditional way of making a risotto is to gently fry the flavourings, add the rice and let it toast in the flavourings and oil, then add boiling stock, little by little, stirring continuously to make the rice creamy, until it is tender and has swelled up to three times its original size from the

The Rules

amount of liquid it has absorbed. Butter and/or parmesan cheese is stirred in vigorously for extra richness. I have used this method in the following recipes – it is one of those satisfying, therapeutic cooking methods that demands time and concentration.

The other method of making risotto is one where stirring continuously is unnecessary as long as you use vialone nano or carnaroli rice. This method involves gently frying off the flavourings, adding the rice and letting it toast. At this point the method differs from the traditional one, as all the boiling stock is added at once, the risotto is brought back to the boil, the heat is lowered and the risotto is covered and simmered for about 15 minutes until the rice is tender. Any other ingredients are added now, the risotto stirred, butter and/or parmesan cheese is added and the risotto is ready. The choice of method is really a matter of personal taste and time.

When making risotto it is important to have a good risotto pan, one that heats evenly and is easy to stir evenly. Another crucial factor is to use good stock. The better the stock the more tasty the risotto.

Risotto is quite a rich dish and, with the exception of the risotto that traditionally accompanies Osso Buco, it is usually served in small amounts as a first course. When a risotto is ready it will not wait – it needs to be eaten immediately.

Roast Chicken Stuffed with Rice and Chinese Mushrooms

This chicken stuffed with sticky rice with Chinese flavours is reminiscent of the famous but complicated Chinese classic, 'Beggar's Chicken'. The chicken is roasted or braised in a covered pan for 2 hours so that it is falling off the bones. The stuffing takes a little time to make, but after that the oven does all the work. The aroma when the chicken is taken out of the oven and carved is stunning. This makes a great dish for a special meal.

Chinese five spice powder and Shao Xing Chinese cooking wine are available at Asian shops.

See also: the Basic Recipe for rice, page 110.

STUFFING

150g (5oz) glutinous white rice
50g (2oz) jasmine or other rice
2 Chinese dried mushrooms
250ml (9fl oz) boiling water
4 cloves garlic
2 tablespoons peanut oil
1 tablespoon finely chopped
    fresh ginger

1/2 teaspoon Chinese five spice
    powder
3 tablespoons Shao Xing Chinese
    cooking wine, or use medium
    dry sherry
1 spring onion
1 teaspoon sugar
3 tablespoons soy sauce

CHICKEN

1.4kg (3lb) organic chicken,
    wing tips cut off
2 tablespoons sesame oil
100ml (31/2 fl oz) of the soaking
    water from the mushrooms
1 tablespoon sugar
2 tablespoons soy sauce

Mix the two varieties of rice, wash them well, soak them for 20 minutes then steam as described in the Basic Recipe on page 110.

Cover the dried mushrooms with the boiling water and soak for at least 20 minutes (or more if they are very thick). Drain and reserve the soaking water. Cut off and discard the stems. Slice the mushroom caps thinly.

Peel and finely chop the garlic. Heat the peanut oil in a wok over a moderate heat and add the garlic, ginger, five spice powder and mushrooms. Stirfry for 3 minutes, without browning. Add the Shao Xing wine and bring to the boil. Trim the ends off the spring onion and slice. Stir in the rice, spring onion, teaspoon of sugar and 3 tablespoons soy sauce and stirfry until the rice is hot and moist. Remove from the heat and let it cool enough to handle.

Preheat the oven to 190°C (375°F). Stuff the chicken using a spoon or your hands. Pin the cavity closed with a bamboo skewer or tie the legs together with string.

Pour the sesame oil, mushroom soaking water, tablespoon of sugar and 2 tablespoons soy sauce into a deep roasting dish and put the chicken in. Cover tightly, either with the lid or with tinfoil, and cook for 11/2 hours, without uncovering, then cook for a further 30 minutes, uncovered, to brown the chicken, basting frequently.

Remove from the oven, skim the fat off the pan juices and serve the chicken and the pan juices straight from the roasting dish. Serve with a mixed vegetable stirfry, steamed white rice and soy sauce and chilli sauces on the side.

SERVES 4–6

Roast Chicken Stuffed with Rice and Chinese Mushrooms

Warm Mussel and Rice Salad

This makes a good first course or light lunch.

500g (1lb 2oz) long grain white rice
1 red onion
1 clove garlic
1 small red capsicum (pepper)
3 tomatoes
100ml (3½ fl oz) extra virgin
    olive oil

2 tablespoons capers
2 tablespoons chopped
    flat-leafed parsley
grated zest of 1 lemon
juice of 2 large lemons
24 medium-sized mussels
125ml (4fl oz) water

salt and freshly ground
    black pepper
10 basil leaves, ripped into
    small pieces

*See also: the
Basic Recipe for
rice, page 110;
and the Basic
Recipe for
mussels, page 10.*

Cook the rice as described in the Basic Recipe on page 110, and let it cool until warm.

Peel and finely chop the onion and garlic. Core and seed the capsicum and thinly slice. Core, halve, seed and thinly slice the tomatoes.

Put the rice into a wide, shallow salad bowl and mix in the extra virgin olive oil, onion, capsicum, tomatoes, capers, parsley, garlic, lemon zest and juice.

Cook the mussels in the water as described in the Basic Recipe on page 10. Time them to be ready with the salad.

When the mussels are cool enough to handle, shell them and add the warm mussels to the salad. Toss gently, taste and season with salt and pepper. Sprinkle basil leaves on top and serve immediately.

SERVES 4–6

Pumpkin and Almond Pilaf with Harissa

This is a great dish to serve with a lamb stew or roast chicken. The rice is flavoured with a slowly cooked sofrito as described in the Basic Recipe on page 99. Basmati and jasmine rice are suitable for this recipe.

Harissa is a North African condiment. Make this first; it will keep for at least 2 weeks in the refrigerator. It is spicy-hot and salty and can be used as a flavour accent for grilled and roasted chicken, meat and fish, as well as in stews.

HARISSA

4 tablespoons coriander seeds
4 tablespoons cumin seeds
100g (3 1/2 oz) fresh red chillies
6 cloves garlic, peeled
4 tablespoons Maldon sea salt
enough extra virgin olive oil to make a paste

PILAF

400g (14oz) long grain white rice
2 tablespoons cumin seeds
300g (10 1/2 oz) peeled and seeded pumpkin
3 cloves garlic
1 onion
4 tablespoons olive oil

1/2 teaspoon ground cinnamon
1 teaspoon ground turmeric
grated zest of 1 orange
1 teaspoon sugar
75g (3oz) chopped roasted almonds
1/2 teaspoon salt
water

See also: The Rules for stew, page 99.

Toast the coriander and cumin seeds separately in a dry pan over a moderate heat until fragrant and just beginning to darken in colour, then grind them to a coarse powder in a mortar – I use an electric coffee grinder reserved just for grinding spices.

Put the toasted coriander and cumin, chillies, garlic and salt into a food processor, adding enough extra virgin olive oil to make a thick paste, and process until smooth. Set aside.

Wash the rice well, soak in plenty of cold water for 20 minutes and drain well. Toast the 2 tablespoons of cumin seeds in a dry pan over a moderate heat. Cut the pumpkin into 2cm (3/4 in) cubes. Peel and finely chop the 3 cloves of garlic and the onion.

Heat the olive oil over a moderate heat and add the garlic, onion, cinnamon, turmeric, orange zest and toasted cumin seeds. Gently fry, without browning, until the onion is soft, as described in The Rules on page 99.

Add the sugar, pumpkin, almonds and rice and mix well. Sauté for 3 minutes, stirring continuously. Add the salt and enough water to cover, and bring to the boil.

Turn the heat down to the lowest setting and cook, without uncovering for any reason, for 20 minutes. Remove from the heat without uncovering and let it stand for 10 minutes. Uncover and fluff up the rice with a fork.

Serve the pilaf on its own or as an accompaniment to meat or chicken and serve the harissa separately. The harissa is eaten as a small dab on top like chilli sauce.

SERVES 4

Lamb Shank Stew with Pumpkin Risotto and Gremolata

One of the few times that risotto is used as an accompaniment is with the famous Italian dish, Osso Buco, braised veal shanks served with saffron flavoured risotto Milanese. The following dish is a similar take, using a fragrant lamb stew with Spanish flavours, which is based on a sofrito but cooked in the oven and served with a pumpkin risotto.
The stew can be made in advance as it reheats well. Your butcher should be able to bone the lamb shanks for you.

See also: *The Rules for stew, page 99; and the Basic Recipe for risotto, page 110.*

LAMB SHANK STEW
4 cloves garlic
1 onion
1 carrot
2 tablespoons olive oil
3 tablespoons currants
1 teaspoon sweet Spanish
    smoked paprika
1/2 teaspoon salt
1/2 teaspoon freshly ground
    black pepper
6 lamb shanks, boned
250ml (9fl oz) well-flavoured
    liquid beef stock

400g (14oz) can Italian whole peeled
    tomatoes in juice, mashed

GREMOLATA
1 large handful flat-leafed parsley
2 cloves garlic
grated zest of 1 lemon

PUMPKIN RISOTTO
400g (14oz) peeled and
    seeded pumpkin
2 cloves garlic
1 onion
3 tablespoons olive oil
grated zest of 1 orange
1/2 teaspoon ground turmeric
400g (14oz) Italian risotto rice
1 litre (1 pint 15fl oz) well-flavoured
    liquid chicken stock
salt and freshly ground
    black pepper
2 tablespoons butter

Preheat the oven to 190°C (375°F). Peel and finely chop the garlic. Peel and chop the onion and carrot.

Heat the 2 tablespoons of olive oil over a moderate heat in a deep saucepan and add the garlic, onion, carrot, currants, paprika, salt and pepper. Gently fry, without browning, until the onion is soft.

Add the boned lamb shanks, stock and tomatoes and mix well. Bring to the boil and cover tightly. Place in the oven and cook for 1 1/2–2 hours, or until the lamb is meltingly tender.

Put the parsley, garlic and lemon zest for the gremolata onto a wooden board and chop it all finely. If you have a semicircular mezzaluna knife, this is the perfect job for it. Set the gremolata aside.

Cut the pumpkin into 2cm (3/4 in) cubes. Peel and finely chop the garlic and onion for the risotto. Heat the 3 tablespoons olive oil over a moderate heat and add the garlic, onion, orange zest, turmeric and pumpkin. Fry gently, without browning, until the onion is soft, as described in The Rules on page 99. Add the rice and gently fry for 3 minutes to 'toast' it, stirring frequently.

Meanwhile, bring the chicken stock to the boil and keep it simmering. Add the stock as described in the Basic Recipe on page 110 and continue until it is all used. Taste some of the rice to check that it is firm to the bite but tender, and season with salt and pepper. Add the butter and mix well.

Have the stew ready and serve it on the risotto with the gremolata sprinkled on top.   SERVES 4–6

Parmesan Risotto with Roasted Vegetables

Put the vegetables in the oven when you start adding the stock to the risotto and they will be ready when the risotto is ready.

ROASTED VEGETABLES

1 carrot

2 courgettes (zucchini)

1 red capsicum (pepper)

100g (3 1/2 oz) green beans

1 clove garlic

8 cherry tomatoes

8 black olives

4 tablespoons extra virgin olive oil

salt and freshly ground
   black pepper

RISOTTO

3 cloves garlic

1 onion

3 tablespoons olive oil

grated zest of 1 lemon

400g (14oz) Italian risotto rice

1 litre (1 pint 15fl oz) well-flavoured
   liquid chicken stock

300g (10 1/2 oz) fresh finely grated
   parmesan cheese plus extra for
   sprinkling on top

salt and freshly ground
   black pepper

2 tablespoons butter

2 tablespoons chopped
   flat-leafed parsley

See also: the Basic Recipe for roasted vegetables, page 88; and the Basic Recipe for risotto, page 110.

Preheat the oven to 200°C (400°F). Peel the carrot, and trim the ends from the carrot and courgettes. Slice the carrot and courgettes lengthways into very thin ribbons. Core, seed and quarter the capsicum. Cut the stalk ends off the beans. Peel and finely chop the garlic.

Put the vegetables and olives into a large, shallow roasting tray, add the garlic and extra virgin olive oil and season well with salt and pepper. Toss everything so that the flavourings and oil are evenly distributed throughout the vegetables. Roast as described in the Basic Recipe on page 88.

Peel and finely chop the garlic and onion for the risotto. Heat the olive oil over a moderate heat and add the garlic, lemon zest and onion. Fry gently, without browning, until the onion is soft. Add the rice and gently fry to 'toast' the rice, stirring frequently.

Meanwhile, bring the chicken stock to the boil and keep it simmering. Add the stock as described in the Basic Recipe on page 110 until it is all used.

Stir in the parmesan cheese and season with salt and pepper to taste. Add the butter and parsley and mix well.

Serve the risotto immediately, garnished with the roasted vegetables and sprinkled with more freshly grated parmesan cheese.

SERVES 4–6

Risotto with Lemon and Fennel

A delicious risotto based on a sofrito of lemon-scented fennel. Don't be scared off by the fennel; there will not be a strong anise flavour from it. The combination with the lemon is subtle and delicious.

1/2 teaspoon saffron
2 fennel bulbs
1 large clove garlic
3 tablespoons extra virgin olive oil
1 tablespoon lemon thyme leaves

grated zest of 2 lemons
400g (14oz) Italian risotto rice
1 litre (1 pint 15fl oz) well-flavoured
    liquid chicken stock
125ml (4fl oz) white wine

juice of 1 large lemon
salt and freshly ground
    black pepper
2 tablespoons butter

See also: The Rules for stew, page 99; and the Basic Recipe for risotto, page 110.

Carefully toast the saffron in a dry frying pan until it darkens slightly and you can smell its fragrance. Remove from the heat and crush to a powder with your fingers or the back of a teaspoon.

Cut the stalks off the fennel, cut out the core, and slice the bulbs thinly. Peel and finely chop the garlic.

Heat the extra virgin olive oil over a moderate heat and add the thyme, garlic, lemon zest, fennel and saffron. Gently fry, without browning, until the fennel has softened, as described in The Rules on page 99. Add the rice, mixing well, and let the rice 'toast' for 3 minutes.

Meanwhile, bring the chicken stock to the boil and keep it simmering. Add the wine to the rice mixture, turn up the heat and let the wine bubble until it is all absorbed. Turn the heat down and add the stock as described in the Basic Recipe on page 110 until it is all used.

Stir in the lemon juice, season with salt and pepper to taste and vigorously stir in the butter.
SERVES 4–6

Risotto with Garden Greens and Bacon

6 silverbeet leaves
1 large clove garlic
3 tablespoons extra virgin olive oil
1 tablespoon thyme leaves
5 rashers rindless bacon, diced

400g (14oz) Italian risotto rice
125ml (4fl oz) white wine
1 litre (1 pint 15fl oz) well-flavoured
    liquid chicken stock
grated zest of 1 lemon
1 large handful each of spinach

and rocket leaves
1 cup chervil sprigs
salt and freshly ground
    black pepper
2 tablespoons butter

See also: The Rules for stew, page 99; and the Basic Recipe for risotto, page 110.

Roughly chop the silverbeet, cook for 5 minutes or until tender in plenty of boiling water, cool under cold water, squeeze dry and chop again. Peel and finely chop the garlic.

Heat the extra virgin olive oil over a moderate heat and add the thyme, garlic and bacon. Gently fry, without browning, as described in The Rules on page 99, until the bacon is cooked. Add the rice and gently fry for 3 minutes to 'toast' it, stirring frequently. Add the wine, turn up the heat, and let the wine bubble until it is all absorbed.

Meanwhile, bring the chicken stock to the boil and keep it simmering. Add the stock as described in the Basic Recipe on page 110 and continue until it is all absorbed. Taste some of the rice to check that it is firm to the bite but tender.

When all the stock is added, stir in the lemon zest, silverbeet, spinach, rocket and chervil, mix carefully, and cook until the silverbeet is hot and the other greens have wilted. Season with salt and pepper and vigorously stir in the butter.

Serve sprinkled with some freshly grated parmesan cheese if desired. **SERVES 4–6**

Dried Pasta

Tender to the bite

Pasta has been enthusiastically adopted by most of us – it's a familiar ingredient in all its forms. While I love it in delicious, traditional Italian dishes, the following recipes are just some of the new ways I like to use good pasta.

Spaghetti with Roast Chicken
  and Salsa Cruda
Roasted Field Mushrooms with
  Lemon and Tarragon Cream
  on Fettuccine
Spaghetti with Roasted Eggplant,
  Lemon, Anchovies and Mint
Vegetable and Bacon Soup
  with Pasta
Steamed Shellfish with Potatoes
  and Onions on Spaghetti
Warm Penne and Roasted
  Vegetable Salad

Basic Recipe

Hot Spaghetti with Parsley, Garlic, Chilli and Olive Oil

This is my 'quick fix' comfort food. Easy to make and good for you, its success relies on good ingredients. Buy the best pasta and olive oil you can afford, and use fresh garlic and parsley.

1¹/₂ tablespoons salt
450g (1lb) Italian spaghetti
2 cloves garlic
¹/₂ small dried red chilli

2 tablespoons finely chopped
flat-leafed parsley
50ml (2fl oz) extra virgin
olive oil

salt and freshly ground
black pepper to taste
freshly grated parmesan cheese
for sprinkling on top

Bring a large saucepan of water to the boil. Add the salt. Stir the pasta into the water and make sure it covers the pasta. Allow the water to return to the boil without boiling over. After about 10 minutes taste a piece or two of pasta to check if it is cooked al dente. If it is not, continue cooking, tasting frequently until it is ready. Drain the pasta and put it into a warm serving bowl.

Peel and finely chop the garlic. Seed and very finely chop the chilli. Add the garlic, chilli, parsley and extra virgin olive oil to the spaghetti and season to taste.

Toss, sprinkle plenty of parmesan cheese on top, and serve immediately.   **SERVES 4**

Pasta is the store cupboard standby that no cook should be without. It is much better to buy Italian dried pasta as it will probably be of better quality than any 'fresh' pasta on the market. Genuine fresh pasta does not keep.

Good quality Italian pasta is not merely a vehicle for the sauce, but an important ingredient made from special hard durum flour and has a delicious flavour of its own. The better quality the pasta the better it will taste. The flavour of good pasta always reminds me of the taste of fresh bread.

The Rules

Cook pasta in plenty of boiling water, at least 4 litres (7 pints) for one 500g (1lb 2oz) packet of dried pasta.

Even if you are cooking less pasta, use almost as much water as you would for a whole packet, so that the pasta has plenty of room to 'swim' around. It must not be crowded in the pan or it will stick together. Increase the amount of water by about 1 litre (1 pint 15fl oz) for every additional 250g (9oz) of pasta. Don't try and cook more than 1kg (2lb 2oz) of pasta in one pot; it is too unwieldy to stir, drain or season.

Salt the water well. Allow 2 tablespoons of salt for 1 packet of pasta.

Never add the pasta until the water has reached a rolling boil and, when you add the pasta, stir it until it comes back to the boil.

Do not break long pasta, wait until it bends and becomes flexible, then push it under the water and stir it in. The water must cover the pasta, no matter what shape you are cooking.

Once the water has returned to the boil, set the heat so that it will continue to boil without boiling over. Pasta must neither be overcooked, or it will be soggy, watery and gluey, nor undercooked, as it will taste raw and unpleasant. It should be cooked 'al dente', or tender but with a slight resistance to the bite.

Only you can tell when pasta is cooked al dente, whatever the manufacturer's instructions say. I can only tell by biting a piece, so I pull some out before I think it will be cooked and keep trying it until I know it is ready.

The minute pasta is cooked it must be drained. Do not let it sit in the water it was cooked in. Once it is drained it needs to be tossed immediately in sauce to stop it sticking together. If this is impossible, it should at least be tossed in a little extra virgin olive oil.

As a general rule, thin light pasta should have thin light sauces. Thicker pasta, especially ridged pasta, can take heavier sauces.

Spaghetti with Roast Chicken and Salsa Cruda

The heat of the pasta and chicken will intensify the fragrance of the salsa.

CHICKEN
1 Basic Recipe Roast Chicken with
   Garlic and Lemon

SALSA CRUDA
6 large ripe tomatoes
3 cloves garlic

See also: the Basic Recipe for chicken, page 48; and The Rules for pasta, page 123.

½ small red onion
125ml (4fl oz) extra virgin olive oil
3 tablespoons balsamic vinegar
1 teaspoon sweet Spanish paprika
12 black olives
salt and freshly ground
   black pepper

SPAGHETTI
450g (1lb) Italian spaghetti
extra virgin olive oil

basil leaves for garnish

Cook the chicken as described in the Basic Recipe on page 48, but do not make the gravy, just carve the chicken.

While the chicken is cooking, prepare the salsa. Core, seed and chop the tomatoes almost to a purée. Peel and finely chop the garlic and onion. Mix all the salsa ingredients together, season to taste, and set aside for 30 minutes.

Cook the spaghetti as described in The Rules on page 123. Toss the spaghetti with a little extra virgin olive oil so that it does not stick together and put it onto a warm serving platter.

Pile the carved chicken on top of the spaghetti and spoon the sauce over everything. Scatter some basil leaves on top and serve immediately.

SERVES 4–6

Roasted Field Mushrooms with Lemon and Tarragon Cream on Fettuccine

The time required to cook the mushrooms will depend on their size and thickness.

See also: The Rules for pasta, page 123.

4 large, flat Portobello (field)
   mushrooms
4 tablespoons olive oil
salt and freshly ground
   black pepper

1 clove garlic
juice and grated zest of 1 lemon
1 tablespoon chopped
   fresh tarragon

2 tablespoons chopped
   fresh chervil
300ml (10½ fl oz) cream
400g (14oz) dried Italian fettuccine
chervil sprigs for garnish

Preheat the oven to 200°C (400°F). Slice the stalks off the mushrooms so they will sit flat. Brush the mushrooms with the olive oil and season well with salt and pepper. Put the mushrooms onto a baking tray and place in the oven for 15 minutes, or until they have softened, just started to brown around the edges and have cooked through. Slice and taste one. It should be moist and tender, but slightly firm to the bite. Put aside and keep them warm.

Peel and finely chop the garlic. Put the garlic, lemon juice and zest, tarragon, chervil and cream into a saucepan and bring to the boil. Turn down the heat and simmer for 2 minutes. Season with salt and pepper to taste. Set aside.

Cook the fettuccine as described in The Rules on page 123. Drain well and put onto a deep, warm serving platter.

Reheat the cream, slice the mushrooms thinly and scatter them over the fettuccine. Pour the cream over everything and scatter chervil sprigs on top.

SERVES 4

Spaghetti with Roasted Eggplant, Lemon, Anchovies and Mint

This dish has the earthy Arab-influenced flavours of Sicily. It makes an elegant but quick and easy first course or light lunch that only needs a green salad to follow it.

1 eggplant, sliced 1cm (1/2 in) thick
olive oil for brushing
salt and freshly ground
     black pepper
3 tablespoons olive oil

1 onion
3 cloves garlic
16 black olives
10 anchovy fillets

grated zest and juice of 1 large
     lemon
400g (14oz) Italian dried spaghetti
mint leaves for garnish

See also: The Rules for stew, page 99; and The Rules for pasta, page 123.

Preheat the oven to 200°C (400°F). Put a large saucepan of well-salted water on to boil for the pasta.

Brush the eggplant slices with plenty of olive oil and sprinkle them well with salt and pepper. Put them in one layer on baking sheets and place in the oven. Roast for about 10 minutes until the underside is well browned, turn, and continue roasting until the other side is brown. Remove from the oven and slice each slice of eggplant into four thick strips. Keep warm.

Peel and finely chop the onion and garlic. Heat the 3 tablespoons of olive oil in a frying pan over a moderate heat and add the onion, garlic, olives, anchovies, lemon juice and lemon zest. Fry gently until the onion is very soft as if you were making a sofrito as described in The Rules on page 99.

Cook the pasta in the boiling water as described in The Rules on page 123.

Add the reserved eggplant and the lemon juice to the onion mix, and mix carefully but well. Taste and season with salt and pepper, but be careful, as the anchovies are salty.

Put the pasta into a warm serving bowl and add the eggplant mixture.

Sprinkle the mint leaves on top and serve.

SERVES 4

Vegetable and Bacon Soup with Pasta

A hearty, filling soup, this is a meal in itself and perfect for cold winter nights.

1 medium-sized waxy potato
200g (7oz) peeled, seeded
    pumpkin
4 cloves garlic
1 onion
1 carrot
4 tablespoons olive oil

3 rashers rindless bacon,
    finely chopped
1 teaspoon finely chopped
    tender rosemary tips
1 stick celery, thinly sliced
150ml (5fl oz) dry white wine
water

salt and freshly ground
    black pepper
1 small handful spinach
    leaves, chopped
1 tablespoon butter
freshly shaved parmesan cheese
    for garnish

See also: The Rules for stew, page 99.

Cut the potato into 2cm (3/4 in) cubes. Cut the pumpkin into 2cm (3/4 in) cubes. Peel and finely chop the garlic and onion. Peel and finely dice the carrot.

Heat the olive oil in a large saucepan over a moderate heat. Add the bacon, garlic, rosemary, onion, carrot, celery, potato and pumpkin. Fry gently, without browning, as described in The Rules on page 99, until the onion is soft.

Add the wine, bring to the boil, and boil until it has almost evaporated. Add enough water to cover the vegetables, season well with salt and pepper, bring to the boil, and simmer until all the vegetables are tender.

Add the spinach and simmer until it is well wilted. Stir in the butter, taste, season again, and serve with shaved parmesan cheese on each portion and plenty of crusty bread.

SERVES 4

Steamed Shellfish with Potatoes and Onions on Spaghetti

3 medium-sized waxy potatoes
3 cloves garlic
3 red onions
4 tablespoons olive oil
1 tablespoon fresh thyme leaves,
    finely chopped

juice and grated zest of 1 lemon
a mixture of any small shellfish
    (mussels, pipis, cockles, clams –
    allow 8 shellfish per person)
100ml (3 1/2 fl oz) dry white wine
400g (14oz) Italian spaghetti

2 tablespoons chopped
    flat-leafed parsley
salt and freshly ground
    black pepper

See also: The Rules for stew, page 99; the Basic Recipe for mussels, page 10; and The Rules for pasta, page 123.

Peel and cut the potatoes into 2cm (3/4 in) dice. Peel and finely chop the garlic. Peel and thinly slice the onions.

Heat the olive oil over a moderate heat and add the garlic, onions, thyme, lemon juice and zest and potatoes. Gently fry, without browning, until the onion is soft as described in The Rules on page 99. Add the seafood and wine, mix well and bring to the boil. Cover and cook as described in the Basic Recipe on page 10 until the shellfish start to open. Uncover the pan and remove the shellfish as they open. By this time the potatoes will be tender.

Cook the spaghetti as described in The Rules on page 123. Time it to be ready when the shellfish is ready.

Stir the parsley into the sofrito, which should now have mixed with the liquor from the shellfish and become a rather thick stew. Taste and season with salt, if necessary, and pepper.

Serve the shellfish and potato on the spaghetti.

SERVES 4

Warm Penne and Roasted Vegetable Salad

As all the vegetables are roasted together, it is important to slice them into similar thicknesses so that they will all cook at the same time.

2 courgettes (zucchini)
2 carrots
10 asparagus spears
200g (7oz) green beans
1 red capsicum (pepper)
4 spring onions
4 cloves garlic

1 teaspoon fennel seeds
12 black olives
100ml (3¹/2 fl oz) extra virgin
    olive oil
salt and freshly ground
    black pepper

250g (9oz) Italian dried penne or
    other short tubular pasta
200g (7oz) feta, crumbled
grated zest of 1 lemon
juice of 2 lemons
extra virgin olive oil for
    sprinkling on top

See also: the Basic Recipe for roasted vegetables, page 88; and The Rules for pasta, page 123.

Preheat the oven to 200°C (400°F). Slice the courgettes and peeled carrots very thinly lengthways. Snap the bottom ends off the asparagus. Trim the stalk ends off the beans. Core, seed, and cut the capsicum into 1cm (¹/2 in) thick slices. Trim the root ends off the spring onions and cut them in half. Peel and thinly slice the garlic.

Put the vegetables, garlic, fennel seeds and olives into a shallow roasting tray. Add the 100ml extra virgin olive oil and season well with salt and pepper. Toss everything so it is evenly coated in oil. Roast the vegetables as described in the Basic Recipe on page 88.

Cook the penne as described in The Rules on page 123. Drain the penne well and put it into a large, warm wide bowl.

Add the roasted vegetables, feta, lemon zest and juice and mix well.

Serve more extra virgin olive oil on the side for people to dribble over their salad if they desire.   SERVES 4–6

Warm Penne and Roasted Vegetable Salad

Asian cool

Dried

While their cooking methods can be similar, don't confuse noodles with pasta. Does one even have to be reminded that Italian pasta can never be substituted for noodles and vice versa? There are many different types of noodles so, if following a recipe, use the noodle appropriate to the cuisine of the dish you are making.

Panfried Fish with Stirfried
    Bok Choy on Egg Noodles
Stirfried Chicken and Pineapple
    with Glass Noodles
Sliced Steak on Egg Noodles
    with Green Thai Dressing
Rice Noodle Salad with Stirfried
    Pork and Chilli Omelette
Steamed Mussels on Egg Noodles
    with Coriander and Sesame Paste

Noodles

Basic Recipe

Chinese Egg Noodles in Chilli Ginger Broth with Tofu

This is a simple dish of cooked noodles in an aromatic chicken broth with cubes of silky tofu. The charm of this dish is its freshness.

Of all Asian ingredients, tofu gets perhaps the worst press among non-Asians who often think it tasteless. Here it is used to give the dish a creamy richness without disturbing the flavours of the herbs. Do not over-boil the broth. Cook it just long enough to infuse the stock and water with the flavour of the herbs. Five minutes usually does it.

200g (7oz) 1/2 cm (1/8 in) thick Chinese egg noodles
1 litre (1 pint 15fl oz) well-flavoured liquid chicken stock
500ml (18fl oz) water

2 small fresh green chillies
3 cloves garlic
2 spring onions
8 paper-thin slices peeled ginger

200g (7oz) firm tofu, cut into 2cm (1in) cubes
soy sauce for seasoning and serving

Bring at least 3 litres (5 pints) of water to the boil and add the noodles. If the noodles are in a flat, cake-like bundle, stir them with a pair of chopsticks or a fork until they soften and separate and the water is boiling again. Boil for 6 minutes.

Taste some of the noodles, being careful not to burn yourself, to see if they are tender. (I usually grab some out of the saucepan with a pair of tongs and run them under the cold tap and then taste them.) Continue cooking until they are tender. Remove from the heat and drain well.

If the noodles are not going into the broth almost immediately, cool them in cold water, drain well, put a couple of tablespoons of soy bean oil on the noodles and toss them gently with your hands so that they do not stick together.

Split the chillies lengthways up to the stalk. Peel the garlic and slice it paper thin. Thinly slice the spring onions on the diagonal. Put the stock, water, garlic, chillies and ginger into a saucepan and bring to the boil. Simmer for 5 minutes then add the noodles. Bring back to the boil and add the tofu. Bring back to the boil again, remove from the heat and divide the noodles, tofu and broth between four bowls. Sprinkle each with some of the spring onions and serve the soy sauce separately. Use the soy sauce to season the noodles and broth.

SERVES 4

The Rules

The popularity of Asian food, especially noodles, is a truly modern phenomenon, so naturally the modern cook should be able to include Asian dishes in his or her cooking repertoire.

In general terms noodles can be divided into the following groups.

- Chinese egg noodles and Japanese ramen noodles, made from wheat flour and eggs. These come in a variety of thicknesses. Boil them in plenty of water until tender like pasta.
- Japanese udon and somen noodles, made from wheat flour, and Japanese soba noodles, made from buckwheat flour or a mixture of buckwheat and wheat flour. Boil in plenty of water until tender, but be careful not to overcook the delicate, thin soba and somen noodles.
- Dried rice noodles, made from rice flour. These should be soaked in hot water to make them flexible, then cooked quickly in boiling water.
- Bean thread noodles, made from mung bean flour. Also called glass noodles, cellophane noodles or lungkow noodles. These should be soaked first, then cooked in boiling water until transparent and tender.

Like pasta, noodles should be cooked in a generous amount of boiling water and given plenty of room in the saucepan. Taste a strand before you think the noodles are cooked, and keep tasting until you feel by biting that they are ready. As soon as they are cooked, drain and use them. Do not let them sit in the cooking water as they will become soggy and overcooked.

Panfried Fish with Stirfried Bok Choy on Egg Noodles

The three simple operations that make up this dish call for a little organisation. Get everything ready before you start.

4 x 200g (7oz) pieces skinned, boned firm white fish fillets
plain flour for dusting
7 tablespoons peanut or soy bean oil

2 cloves garlic
3cm (1in) piece peeled fresh ginger
6 baby bok choy
4 tablespoons oyster sauce

350g (12$\frac{1}{2}$ oz) thin Chinese egg noodles
soy sauce
sweet chilli sauce

See also: the Basic Recipe for fish, page 70.

Put a large saucepan of water on to boil for the noodles.

Dust the fish in the flour and shake off the excess. Using 4 tablespoons of the soy bean oil, panfry the fish as described in the Basic Recipe on page 70.

While the fish is finishing in the oven, prepare the ingredients for stirfrying. Peel and thinly slice the garlic. Slice the ginger very thinly. Remove the coarse outer leaves and slice the bok choy into quarters lengthways. Heat a wok over a high heat, add the remaining 3 tablespoons of soy bean oil and then add the garlic and ginger. Stirfry for 10 seconds then add the bok choy. Keep the temperature on high and stirfry the bok choy until it looks wilted and translucent. Taste a small piece – it should be hot and cooked but crunchy. Add the oyster sauce, mix well and remove from the heat.

Add the noodles to the boiling water and stir until they separate and the water comes back to the boil. Boil for 4 minutes, then taste some of the noodles and continue tasting until the noodles are tender but not overcooked. Remove from the heat and drain well.

Serve a piece of fish on some of the noodles in a large bowl with some of the bok choy on the side. Serve soy sauce and sweet chilli sauce separately in small bowls.

Use chopsticks to eat this if you are comfortable with them – the fish will break up easily and noodles are easier to eat with chopsticks.

SERVES 4

Stirfried Chicken and Pineapple with Glass Noodles

Glass noodles are also called cellophane noodles, lungkow noodles or bean thread noodles. They are dry and tough when you buy them and are best cut with scissors. They soften after soaking and can then be cooked.

Pay attention to the stirfrying part of this dish. Make sure the heat is high so that the food in the wok doesn't stew. You should hear the food stirfrying and smell the 'wok aroma' of the food cooking.

200g (7oz) glass noodles
600g (1lb 5oz) skinned, boneless organic chicken breast
1/2 pineapple
4 spring onions
4 cloves garlic

4 tablespoons peanut oil
3 tablespoons finely chopped fresh ginger
1 small fresh green chilli, thinly sliced
1 teaspoon sugar

3 tablespoons fish sauce
10 mint leaves for garnish
soy sauce

Soak the noodles in hot water for 10 minutes or until soft and flexible. Put a large saucepan of water on to boil for the noodles.

Slice the chicken thinly across the grain of the meat. Peel and core the pineapple and cut into bite-sized chunks. Trim the ends off the spring onions and cut into 3cm (1 1/2 in) pieces. Peel and thinly slice the garlic.

Heat the peanut oil in a wok until hot but not smoking. Add the garlic, ginger and chilli and stirfry for 20 seconds without burning it. Add the chicken and stirfry over a high heat until well browned.

Add the sugar, fish sauce, pineapple and spring onions to the wok and stirfry over a high heat until very hot and the chicken is cooked.

Drain the noodles from the soaking water, add them to the boiling water and boil for 5 minutes, or until they become transparent.

Remove the noodles from the heat, drain well and put then into a large, shallow serving dish.

Sprinkle the chicken and pineapple mixture onto the noodles and sprinkle the mint leaves on top. Serve with soy sauce on the side.

SERVES 4

Sliced Steak on Egg Noodles with Green Thai Dressing

This dish is like a hot noodle and beef salad comprising three simple layers of tastes and textures that go together well. When you are shopping for palm sugar (available from Asian food stores), choose the dark, hard kind called Gula Melacca.
Rump, eye fillet, rib eye or sirloin steak are all suitable cuts. The weight given is the trimmed weight, after all the fat and sinew has been removed.

See also: The Rules for steak, page 59; and the Basic Recipe for noodles, page 132.

GREEN THAI DRESSING
3 small fresh green chillies
5 spring onions
5 large cloves garlic
3cm (1 1/2 in) long piece peeled
    fresh ginger, chopped
1 large handful coriander leaves
    and stalks

150g (5oz) grated palm sugar
200ml (7fl oz) fresh lime or lemon
    juice
1 teaspoon salt

STEAK AND NOODLES
2 cloves garlic
4 tablespoons peanut oil

1 teaspoon sugar
2 tablespoons fish sauce
600g (1lb 5oz) piece steak
350g (12 1/2 oz) 1/2 cm (1/8 in) thick
    Chinese egg noodles
75g (3oz) finely chopped roasted
    unsalted peanuts

Cut the stalk ends off the chillies, split them lengthways and remove the seeds. Trim off the ends and chop the spring onions. Peel and chop the garlic. Put all the dressing ingredients into a food processor and purée until smooth. Taste and add more salt if necessary. Reserve.

Preheat the oven to 200°C (400°F). Put a large saucepan of water on to boil for the noodles.

Peel the garlic and crush to a paste. Mix the peanut oil, sugar, fish sauce and garlic and rub it all over the piece of steak. Heat a frying pan until very hot, add the steak and the oil mixture and brown it all over. Put the steak into the oven to finish cooking, turning it occasionally. Cook for 15 minutes for medium rare, or for less time as desired. Use the touch test as described in The Rules on page 59 to decide when it is cooked. Remove from the oven and let it rest in a warm place for 10 minutes while you cook the noodles.

Add the noodles to the boiling water, stir until they separate, soften and the water comes back to the boil. Boil for 6 minutes, taste them to check they are tender as described in the Basic Recipe on page 132. Remove from the heat and drain.

Put the noodles into a large, wide shallow bowl. Slice the steak thinly and put it on top of the noodles. Pour the dressing over the steak and sprinkle the chopped peanuts on top. Serve immediately. **SERVES 4–6**

Rice Noodle Salad with Stirfried Pork and Chilli Omelette

Cold sweet and sour rice noodle salads are a favourite of mine, especially when the weather is hot. The combination of chilled slippery rice noodles and hot stirfried pork is delicious. Make the chilli omelette first as it is used cold.

See also: the Basic Recipe for omelettes, page 18.

CHILLI OMELETTE
1 spring onion
4 eggs
2 (or more to taste) small dried red chillies, thinly sliced
2 tablespoons soy sauce

NOODLE SALAD
250g (9oz) flat, wide dried rice noodles
1/2 cucumber
1 small carrot
2 spring onions
3 cloves garlic

150g (5oz) asparagus
grated zest of 1 lemon
75g (3oz) chopped unsalted roasted peanuts
3 tablespoons fish sauce
3 tablespoons sugar
1 tablespoon Japanese soy sauce
1 tablespoon peanut oil
4 tablespoons rice vinegar

STIRFRIED PORK
2 cloves garlic
400g (14oz) pork fillet, all fat and sinew removed

3 tablespoons peanut oil
2 tablespoons finely chopped fresh ginger
2 tablespoons fish sauce
1 tablespoon sugar

GARNISH
6 basil leaves, ripped into small pieces
6 mint leaves, ripped into small pieces
2 tablespoons finely chopped coriander leaves

Trim and thinly slice the spring onion. Lightly beat the eggs, mix the eggs, chillies, soy sauce and spring onion together and make the omelette as described in the Basic Recipe on page 18, omitting the herbs. When it is ready, transfer it from the pan onto a wooden board, fold it in half and let it cool. Once cool, slice it thinly. Put the omelette slices on a plate and set aside.

Soak the noodles in hot water for 10 minutes or until soft and flexible.

Peel the cucumber, split lengthways, scrape out the seeds with a teaspoon and cut the flesh into 1cm (1/2 in) cubes. Peel the carrot and shave it down to nothing with a potato peeler so that you have lots of very thin carrot ribbons. Trim and thinly slice the spring onions. Peel and finely chop the garlic for the salad.

Snap the bottom ends off the asparagus, drop the spears into boiling water for 3 minutes, cool in cold water and drain. Cut each spear into three slices on the diagonal.

Drain the soaked noodles and drop them into a large saucepan of boiling water. Let them come back to the boil and taste a few to make sure they are tender. Remove from the heat and drain. They do not take long to cook.

Cool the noodles under cold running water and drain well. Put them into a large bowl and add the remaining salad ingredients. Toss gently so as not to break up the noodles. Set aside.

Peel and finely chop the garlic for the pork. Slice the pork thinly across the grain of the meat. Heat the peanut oil in a wok until hot but not smoking. Add the ginger and garlic and stirfry for 10 seconds. Add the pork, fish sauce and sugar and stirfry over a high heat until the pork is cooked through and the mixture is dry and well browned.

Serve the hot stirfried pork on top of the salad, the omelette sprinkled on top of the pork and the herb garnish sprinkled over everything.

SERVES 4

Steamed Mussels on Egg Noodles with Coriander and Sesame Paste

Take care not to overcook the mussels and noodles. When you have a dish with such simple components, it is impossible to hide anything not cooked well.

CORIANDER AND SESAME PASTE

4 tablespoons sesame seeds
3 cloves garlic
75g (3oz) roasted unsalted peanuts
1 large handful coriander sprigs
   (stalks and leaves)
2 tablespoons sesame oil
150ml (5fl oz) peanut oil
1/2 teaspoon salt

MUSSELS AND NOODLES

24 medium-sized mussels
125ml (4fl oz) well-flavoured
   liquid chicken stock
350g (12 1/2 oz) thick Chinese
   egg noodles

See also: The Rules and Basic Recipe for mussels, page 10; and the Basic Recipe for noodles, page 132.

Toast the sesame seeds in a dry pan over a moderate heat until you can smell their fragrance, see them darken in colour and see and hear them start to pop. Transfer them from the pan immediately to a cold plate, otherwise they will continue cooking in the pan and burn.

Peel and chop the garlic. Put the sesame seeds, peanuts, coriander, garlic, sesame oil, peanut oil and salt into a food processor and process until smooth. Set aside.

Clean the mussels as described in The Rules on page 10. Put the mussels and chicken stock into a large saucepan and cook the mussels as described in the Basic Recipe on page 10.

Cook the noodles as described in the Basic Recipe on page 132.

Serve the mussels on the noodles with the liquid from the mussels poured over them. Serve the Coriander and Sesame Paste separately. Let everyone help themselves to a spoonful of the paste to put on top of the mussels and noodles. As you eat, the paste flavours the mussels and noodles.   **SERVES 4**

Smack your lips

Pound Cake

Everyone should be able to make a cake, especially a pound cake. Giving someone a cake is the perfect way to say 'Welcome', 'Sorry', 'Happy Birthday', 'Congratulations' or 'We're thinking of you'. It shows that you have given the things that are perceived as the most valuable these days, your time and skill. Pound cake also makes a lip-smacking dessert.

Warm Chocolate Chip Pound Cakes with Laurie's Raspberry Compote and Clotted Cream

Toasted Pound Cake with Fresh Berries and Greek Yoghurt

Coconut Pound Cake with Banana Semifreddo

Lemon Syrup Pound Cake with Roasted Peaches

Orange and Polenta Pound Cake with Prune and Port Semifreddo

Basic Recipe

Pound Cake

200g (7oz) unsalted butter	finely grated zest of 1 lemon	250g (9oz) plain flour
350g (12 1/2 oz) castor sugar	5 eggs	icing sugar for dusting

Preheat the oven to 180°C (350°F). Butter a 20cm (8in) diameter loose-bottomed cake tin and line the bottom with greaseproof paper.

Cream the butter, castor sugar and lemon zest with vigorous beating until pale and fluffy.

Beat the eggs in, one at a time, beating well after each addition. Stir in the flour until well mixed, but do not beat.

Pour the mixture into the tin and bake for 45 minutes to 1 hour, until a bamboo skewer inserted into the middle of the cake comes out clean with no wet cake mixture adhering to it.

Remove the cake from the oven and let it cool. Remove from the tin and liberally dust the top of the cake with a blizzard of icing sugar.

Serve the cake in wedges with mascarpone or whipped cream, and a glass of sweet dessert wine. It's also very good with coffee. **SERVES 6–8**

The Rules

Pound cake is a favourite of mine and is a cake that can be pulled and twisted to take on many flavours and perform many functions. It is also an old-fashioned cake that doesn't rely on baking powder to rise.

Originally, pound cake was made from a pound each of butter, sugar, eggs and flour, hence the name. These days the mixture is lighter but it is still a plain, rather dense cake, one that never fails to surprise me because it has a pleasing, intense fresh flavour I never expect from something that looks so unassuming. It will keep for a week in an airtight tin.

You can smell this cake when it is ready to come out of the oven. Your kitchen will be filled with a fresh, buttery, baking aroma that usually means the cake is done.

If you decide you are a cake-maker or a baker, it is probably worth investing in an electric mixer. Creaming butter and sugar, whipping egg whites and kneading bread dough are child's play with the help of technology. I have a reliable old mixer with a metal bowl, which stands on my kitchen bench and makes baking easy.

A cake is the result of a successful chemical reaction and, for this to work, accurate measuring of ingredients is crucial. Unlike other dishes you can't 'tweak' a cake by adding something halfway through cooking. For someone who enjoys baking a precise set of scales is essential.

Warm Chocolate Chip Pound Cakes with Laurie's Raspberry Compote and Clotted Cream

Laurie Black, an architect turned chef, worked with me at Metropole restaurant in Auckland where she dreamt up this delicious compote.

LAURIE BLACK'S RASPBERRY COMPOTE
375g (13½ oz) castor sugar
500g (1lb 2oz) fresh or frozen
    raspberries
125ml (4fl oz) water
juice and grated zest of 1 lemon
clotted cream for serving

CHOCOLATE CHIP POUND CAKES
1 Basic Recipe Pound Cake, but
    omit the lemon zest
1 teaspoon pure vanilla extract
150g (5oz) chocolate chips

Put the castor sugar, half the raspberries, the water, lemon juice and zest into a saucepan and bring to the boil. Boil until syrupy and remove from the heat. Cool completely, add the remaining raspberries and mix carefully. Chill.

Make the Basic Recipe for Pound Cake on the opposite page, but replace the lemon zest with vanilla extract and stir in the chocolate chips with the flour.

Instead of baking the cake in a large tin, butter and paper 6 x 200ml (7fl oz) capacity ramekins and pour the mixture evenly into them. Bake for 30 minutes or until a skewer comes out clean when inserted into the middle of one. Remove from the oven and, when cool enough to handle, remove from the ramekins.

Serve each warm pound cake with some of the raspberry compote and a dollop of clotted cream on top.

SERVES 6

Toasted Pound Cake with Fresh Berries and Greek Yoghurt

Turn the pound cake into a hot pudding.

1 Basic Recipe Pound Cake
4 tablespoons icing sugar
juice of 1 orange
500g (1lb 2oz) fresh mixed berries
    of your choice
350g (12½ oz) thick, creamy
    Greek yoghurt

Make the Basic Recipe for Pound Cake on the opposite page, but bake it in a 13 x 24cm (5 x 9½ in) loaf tin instead of a round tin.

Check to see if it is cooked after 40 minutes. Remove the cake from the oven and let it cool completely.

Remove from the tin and slice into 3cm (1in) thick slices and toast them on each side under a grill until golden brown.

Put the icing sugar, orange juice and berries into a bowl and mix gently but well.

Serve the warm toasted pound cake with plenty of fresh berries and a dollop of Greek yoghurt.

SERVES 6–8

The Rules

Semifreddo

A semifreddo is a way of making something as good as ice cream without an expensive ice cream machine. As it is made with fresh eggs, it doesn't keep like ice cream so make it early on the day you need it or, at the most, the day before. A variety of flavours can be added. See the following recipes for ideas.

The main thing to pay attention to when making a semifreddo is the folding of the mixtures together. What will stop it freezing into an indestructible ice block that is difficult to scoop is the amount of air in the mixture. The beating of the eggs and sugar, and the cream is designed to put air into the mixture and keep it

soft as it freezes. If you are heavy-handed when folding the mixtures together, all the air will be squashed out. A good folding technique is crucial. Use a metal spoon; wooden and plastic spoons have a blunt edge that will squash out the air.

Once the mixtures are in the same bowl, push the spoon to the bottom and lift a large spoonful to the top, pouring it over everything.

Repeat the process, rotating the bowl so that the bottom is lifted and poured over the top. Keep going until the mixture looks well mixed but is still as bulky as when you started. Take your time, folding can't be hurried.

Coconut Pound Cake with Banana Semifreddo

See also: the Basic Recipe for pound cake, page 142.

BANANA SEMIFREDDO
4 eggs
150g (5oz) castor sugar
3 bananas, mashed
juice of 1 lemon
2 tablespoons castor sugar, extra
350ml (12½ fl oz) cream

COCONUT POUND CAKE
1 Basic Recipe Pound Cake
75g (3oz) long strand coconut
3 tablespoons long strand coconut
   for sprinkling on top

400ml (14fl oz) thick canned
   coconut cream

Beat the eggs and castor sugar for the semi-freddo until pale, thick and at least quadrupled in bulk.

In another bowl beat the bananas, lemon juice and 2 tablespoons of castor sugar together until smooth.

In a third bowl, whip the cream until stiff but not buttery.

Fold the three mixtures together, pour into a container and freeze for a minimum of 5 hours or maximum overnight. If frozen overnight,

remove from the freezer 5–10 minutes before serving and let it soften slightly.

Make the Basic Recipe for Pound Cake on page 142, but stir the 75g coconut in with the flour, and sprinkle the 3 tablespoons coconut over the top of the mixture before baking. Bake as usual.

Serve each person a wedge of cake with a scoop of semifreddo and thick coconut cream poured over the top.   SERVES 6–8

Coconut Pound Cake with Banana Semifreddo

Lemon Syrup Pound Cake with Roasted Peaches

POUND CAKE
1 Basic Recipe Pound Cake
grated zest of 1 extra lemon

LEMON SYRUP
400g (14oz) sugar
250ml (9fl oz) water
grated zest of 1 lemon
juice of 3 lemons

ROASTED PEACHES
6 large peaches
juice of 1 orange
juice of 1 lemon
6 tablespoons castor sugar

Make the Basic Recipe for Pound Cake on page 142, using the finely grated zest of 2 lemons instead of the zest of 1 lemon. Bake as usual. Let the cake cool and put it into a wide platter with sides.

Put the sugar, water, lemon zest and juice into a saucepan and bring to the boil, stirring to dissolve the sugar. Boil for 2 minutes. Remove from the heat. Pour the syrup over the cool cake and keep spooning the syrup over the cake as it soaks it up. Put into the refrigerator and chill.

Preheat the oven to 190°C (375°F). Peel and halve the peaches, carefully cutting the stone away from the flesh. Put the peach halves into a small roasting dish. Pour the fruit juices over the top and sprinkle with the castor sugar. Place in the oven and roast for 20–30 minutes until browned and tender but not collapsing. Remove from the oven.

Serve the cake in wedges with some of the hot or warm roasted peaches and whipped cream, clotted cream or Greek yoghurt.

SERVES 6–8

See also: the Basic Recipe for pound cake, page 142.

Orange and Polenta Pound Cake with Prune and Port Semifreddo

I like the crunchy texture the polenta gives the cake and the nougaty texture of the semifreddo.

SEMIFREDDO
200g (7oz) soft pitted prunes
100ml (3½ fl oz) port
4 eggs
150g (5oz) castor sugar
350ml (12½ fl oz) cream

ORANGE AND POLENTA POUND CAKE
1 Basic Recipe Pound Cake, but
    omit the lemon zest
finely grated zest of 2 oranges
juice of ½ orange
100g (3½ oz) polenta

See also: The Rules for semifreddo, page 144; and the Basic Recipe for pound cake, page 142.

Thinly slice the prunes and mix the prunes and port together. Set aside for 1 hour. Beat the eggs and castor sugar until pale, thick and at least quadrupled in bulk. In another bowl, whip the cream until stiff but not buttery.

Fold the prunes, egg mixture and whipped cream together, pour into a container and freeze for a minimum of 5 hours or maximum overnight. If frozen overnight, remove from the freezer 5–10 minutes before serving to let it soften slightly.

Make the Basic Recipe for Pound Cake on page 142, but use the finely grated zest of 2 oranges instead of the lemon zest. Add the orange juice with the last egg. Stir the polenta in with the flour. Bake as usual.

Serve each person a wedge of cake with a scoop of semifreddo.

SERVES 6–8

Lemon Syrup Pound Cake with Roasted Peaches

Colour, fragrance, flavour

Fruit

The paramount consideration when buying fruit, as with all ingredients, is to buy the best quality you can afford. Buy fruit in the quantities you are going to use and buy it ripe so that it will taste at its peak.

Roasted Fruit Salad with Red
    Wine and Frozen Muscovado
    Greek Yoghurt
Berry Trifle with Mascarpone
Summer Pound Cake Pudding
Strawberry and Dried Fruit
    Salad with White Chocolate
    Semifreddo
Tropical Fruit Salad with
    Passionfruit Semifreddo and
    Macadamia Pound Cake

Fruit Salad

Basic Recipe

This is more of a method than a recipe!

Take enough fresh fruit for four people, choosing the fruit with regard to its colours, flavours and fragrance, and make sure these are varied and interesting. If apples and oranges are the only thing available, then fruit salad is not really an option.

Peel and slice the fruit where necessary – for example remove furry peach skins and, if the skin on the pears is papery, then that should go as well.

Dress the fruit with a good dusting of icing sugar and freshly squeezed orange juice. On the day of the photo shoot for this book, my basic fruit salad recipe contained pink grapefruit, pears, oranges, grapes, strawberries, watermelon, peaches, plums and nectarines.

If I had not been able to find a good selection to make an interesting fruit salad, I would have chosen the one variety of fruit I could find which was at its best and simply used that. Imagine a stunning bowl of scarlet plums glistening with sugar and orange juice.

Serve fruit salad with one of the following: whipped cream, clotted cream, crème fraîche, Greek yoghurt or mascarpone, and you will have a sweet course that is simple, yet if made carefully, exquisite!   **SERVES 4**

The Rules

No cook can ignore the colour, fragrance and above all the flavour of fruit. There is a voluptuousness about sweet, juicy fruit that has great appeal.

When making a fruit salad, don't slice the fruit too small. The less handled the more appetising it looks. Try to slice it so that it in some way reminds you of the fruit's original shape.

As a general rule I tend to keep tropical fruit separate from other fruit, although not always.

I don't get hysterical about seasonality when buying fruit; I just try not to buy artificially raised fruit. If it grew naturally on the other side of the world, I don't see why I shouldn't take advantage of the airfreight miracle and enjoy it if I feel like it.

Roasted Fruit Salad with Red Wine and Frozen Muscovado Greek Yoghurt

The frozen yoghurt is a variation on a semifreddo, but instead of using cream you use thick Greek yoghurt so that you get a tart, sour semifreddo to go with the sweet hot fruit. Muscovado sugar is a less refined dark sugar with a treacly taste and is available from supermarkets.

FROZEN MUSCOVADO GREEK YOGHURT
4 eggs
finely grated zest of 1 orange
250g (9oz) dark
   muscovado sugar
350ml (12^1/$_2$ fl oz) thick, Greek-
   style yoghurt, well beaten

ROASTED FRUIT SALAD
3 nectarines
1 apple
^{1}/$_2$ pineapple
small bunch of seedless grapes
6 dried figs, halved
2 candied orange slices, chopped
10 fresh dates, stoned

125g (4^1/$_2$ oz) white sugar
200ml (7fl oz) red wine
icing sugar for dusting

Beat the eggs, orange zest and three-quarters of the muscovado sugar until pale, fluffy and quadrupled in bulk. Fold the yoghurt into the egg mixture. Crumble the remaining muscovado sugar and stir it into the mixture.

Pour the mixture into one large container, or into eight 100ml (3^1/$_2$ fl oz) capacity individual moulds.

Freeze for a minimum of 5 hours or maximum overnight. If freezing overnight, remove it from the freezer 5–10 minutes before serving to let it soften slightly.

Preheat the oven to 200°C (400°F). Stone and quarter the nectarines. Peel, core and slice the apple. Peel and core the pineapple and cut into chunks. Detach the grapes from their stem. Put the nectarines, apple, pineapple, grapes, figs, orange slices, dates, white sugar and red wine into a shallow roasting dish, mix well and bake for 25 minutes.

Remove from the oven, dust with icing sugar, and serve the hot fruit salad with a scoop of the Frozen Muscovado Greek Yoghurt.

SERVES 6–8

Berry Trifle with Mascarpone

Trifle given an Italian twist using your own pound cake.

1 Basic Recipe Pound Cake
150ml (5fl oz) sweet sherry
  or Marsala
150g (5oz) raspberry jam

500g (1lb 2oz) mixed fresh berries
juice of 1 orange
200g (7oz) mascarpone
300ml (10½ fl oz) cream

100g (3½ oz) best quality dark
  chocolate, finely chopped

See also: the Basic Recipe for pound cake, page 142.

Make the Basic Recipe for Pound Cake as described on page 142. Slice the cake up into 1cm (½ in) thick slices and line the bottom of a large, wide shallow bowl with it. Sprinkle the sherry or Marsala over the cake. Spread the jam over the cake.

Put a quarter of the berries and the orange juice into a bowl and mash the berries. Add the remaining berries and mix well. Pour the berry mixture over the cake. Spread the mascarpone on top.

Whip the cream into soft peaks and spread it on top of the mascarpone. Sprinkle the chocolate on top. SERVES 6–8

Summer Pound Cake Pudding

Best made a day in advance, Summer Pudding is usually made with stale bread, but made with pound cake you get a much richer, sweeter pudding. The fruit filling is my own interpretation of the usual berry filling and is like a cooked fruit salad.

1 Basic Recipe Pound Cake
5 large sticks rhubarb

juice and grated zest of 1 orange
250g (9oz) sugar

250ml (9fl oz) red wine
500g (1lb 2oz) mixed berries

See also: the Basic Recipe for pound cake, page 142.

Make the Basic Recipe for Pound Cake as described on page 142.

Trim the rhubarb and cut into 3cm lengths. Put the rhubarb, orange juice and zest, sugar and red wine into a saucepan and bring to the boil. Simmer until the rhubarb is tender. Add the berries, bring back to the boil, then remove from the heat and cool.

Line a 1.25 litre (2 pint) capacity bowl with a large piece of plastic food wrap.

Slice the pound cake into 1cm (½ in) thick slices and neatly line the bottom and sides of the bowl with them so there are no gaps. Pour in one-third of the fruit mixture and top with a layer of cake. Add another third of the fruit mixture and top with a layer of cake. Add the final third of the fruit mixture and finish with a layer of cake.

Place on top a small plate or saucer that will fit inside the rim of the bowl. Cover loosely with plastic food wrap and weight lightly. Refrigerate overnight.

Next day turn the pudding out onto a plate and serve wedges with mascarpone, clotted cream or whipped cream. SERVES 6–8

Strawberry and Dried Fruit Salad with White Chocolate Semifreddo

The combination of the cooked dried fruit and spices with the raw strawberries is truly delicious.

WHITE CHOCOLATE SEMIFREDDO

200g (7oz) good quality white chocolate

4 eggs

75g (3oz) castor sugar

3 tablespoons white crème de cacao or brandy

350ml (12¹/₂ fl oz) cream

STRAWBERRY AND DRIED FRUIT SALAD

125g (4¹/₂ oz) brown sugar

200g (7oz) mixed dried fruit such as currants, raisins, sliced apricots, sliced prunes, etc

grated zest and juice of 1 orange

125ml (4fl oz) red wine

1 cinnamon stick

¹/₄ teaspoon coarsely ground cardamom seeds

500g (1lb 2oz) hulled strawberries

See also:
The Rules for semifreddo, page 144.

Finely grate half of the chocolate and chop the other half.

Beat the eggs and castor sugar until pale, thick and at least quadrupled in bulk.

In another bowl whip the cream and crème de cacao or brandy until stiff but not buttery. Fold the egg mixture, cream and chocolate together and pour into a container.

Freeze for a minimum of 5 hours or maximum overnight. If freezing overnight, remove it from the freezer 5–10 minutes before serving to let it soften slightly.

Put the brown sugar, your selection of dried fruit, orange zest and juice, wine, cinnamon and cardamom into a saucepan and bring to the boil.

Turn the heat down and simmer for 3 minutes. Remove the saucepan from the heat and let it cool. Stir the strawberries into the mixture and chill.

Serve each person a scoop or two of the semifreddo with a big spoonful of the fruit salad.

SERVES 6–8

Tropical Fruit Salad with Passionfruit Semifreddo and Macadamia Pound Cake

This has all my favourite South Pacific flavours. If these fruits are not available, choose any combination of tropical fruits to serve six people.

MACADAMIA POUND CAKE
1 Basic Recipe Pound Cake, but
   omit the lemon zest
seeds scraped out of 1 vanilla bean
150g (5oz) macadamia nuts

PASSIONFRUIT SEMIFREDDO
4 eggs
250g (9oz) castor sugar

pulp from 6 large passionfruit
juice of 1/2 lemon
350ml (12 1/2 fl oz) cream

TROPICAL FRUIT SALAD
2 cardamom pods
1/2 pineapple
1/2 Fijian pawpaw (papaya)
1 mango

2 kiwifruit or golden kiwifruit
4 feijoas
200g (7oz) sugar
125ml (4fl oz) water
grated zest of 1 lemon
1 kaffir lime leaf
1 cinnamon stick
1 banana, sliced

See also: the Basic Recipe for pound cake, page 142; and The Rules for semifreddo, page 144.

Make the Basic Recipe for Pound Cake on page 142 but omit the lemon zest. Add the vanilla bean seeds to the butter and sugar, and cream as in the recipe. Add the macadamia nuts with the flour and bake as usual.

Beat the eggs and castor sugar for the semifreddo until pale, thick and at least quadrupled in bulk.

In another bowl mix the passionfruit pulp and lemon juice.

In a third bowl whip the cream until thick but not buttery. Fold the contents of the three bowls together and freeze for a minimum of 5 hours or maximum overnight. If freezing overnight, remember to remove it from the freezer 5–10 minutes before serving to let it soften slightly.

Squash and bruise the cardamom pods. Peel and core the pineapple and cut the flesh into chunks. Peel, seed and thinly slice the pawpaw. Peel the mango, cut the flesh away from the seed and slice it. Peel and slice the kiwifruit. Halve the feijoas and scoop the flesh out with a teaspoon.

Put the sugar, water, lemon zest, cardamom pods, lime leaf and cinnamon stick into a saucepan. Bring to the boil and boil for 2 minutes. Remove from the heat, cool then chill. Remove the spices and lime leaf and discard them.

Put all the fruit into a bowl and pour the syrup over the fruit. Mix gently but well.

Serve each person a wedge of cake with a scoop of semifreddo and some fruit salad. If desired, serve a jug of coconut cream on the side.
SERVES 6–8

Tropical Fruit Salad with Passionfruit Semifreddo and Macadamia Pound Cake

What a cook needs

To produce good food you really don't need much more than a sharp knife or two, a board to work on, pots and pans, water, heat and top-quality ingredients. (I find that a glass or two of good wine and loud music are excellent optional extras.) But most of us love cooking tools and besides, I don't know anyone who ever regretted buying a professional wooden chopping board or a granite mortar.

The same applies to knives – don't stint on these. Ideally your knife kit should include a steel for sharpening, a large knife (25cm long blade), a small knife (10cm long blade), and a bread knife. Buy other knives as you find you need them, and learn how to get the best out of them. Good knives are worth being fanatical about. Keep them sharp, keep them out of the dishwasher (rattling around in a heavy wash cycle will blunt them), and keep them out of other people's hands so that you're sure they are always well looked after.

It's not essential to have absolutely everything you're ever going to need in the pantry. Good cooks plan ahead as much as possible. That way you can always go and buy what you need. However, the more you cook the faster you will build up a store cupboard of the things that are useful to have at hand.

Although the range of good-quality natural ingredients is constantly widening, and can therefore be bewildering, always try to buy the best you can find. This doesn't have to mean the most expensive if you know what to look for. Apart from what it looks like, use your sense of smell and touch to guide you towards choosing the best ingredients for the job. As shopkeepers rarely encourage customers to handle their produce, you need to remember why something was good in order to build up a series of benchmarks of excellence for the next time you go shopping. This includes paying attention to which brands of packaged ingredients give the best results. And once you've got your shopping home, you need to keep it in prime condition until you use it.

The following list is not intended to be exhaustive, but it provides some tips on useful ingredients to have at hand and how best to store them.

Herbs

As most dried herbs have a characteristic 'dried herb' taste, I always use fresh herbs, the only exception being tarragon. Grow a range of fresh herbs yourself if you can. But if you do have to buy them, ensure they are healthy and lush looking with intact branches. Store them carefully in the container they came in or in plastic bags in the crisper section of the refrigerator.

Spices

Buy these in small quantities and grind them when you need them – it may sound/be tedious but the difference between pre-ground and freshly ground spice is astonishing. Store spices in airtight containers out of the light.

Vegetables and fruit

Try to buy fresh produce in peak condition, not under- or overripe. It should be firm with a good colour. Avoid anything peeled or cut as this will affect the taste and nutritional value. A good supply of fresh ginger, lemons and garlic are useful stock items.

Meat and poultry

Organic poultry and a good range of organic meat cuts are now widely available. However, butchering is a skilled job so meat and poultry shouldn't be carelessly cut or presented. In particular, chicken should look plump and moist, without any discoloured patches or tears in the skin. Buy from a shopkeeper you trust to ensure good quality. Raw meat should be covered and stored on the lower shelves of the refrigerator so that it doesn't drip on (and possibly contaminate) cooked food.

Fish

Choose fish that is plump, rosy or pearly white – depending on the variety – with the aroma of fresh seawater, rather than a strong fishy smell. If you are buying whole fish, ensure the eyes are still plump and shiny. A look under the gills should reveal a rosy red colour. Buy fish as close as possible to the time you plan to cook it as it doesn't keep well. When you get it home, wipe the fish with a damp cloth and store, covered, in the refrigerator until needed.

Soy sauce

Soy sauce is one of those ingredients that must be specific to the food it is used with – in other words use Japanese soy sauce for Japanese cooking and Chinese soy sauce for Chinese cooking (I also recommend that you have both light and dark Chinese soy sauce available). Refrigerate soy sauce after opening.

Oil

I recommend that you keep a range of oils on hand including peanut oil, canola oil, commercially blended extra virgin olive for cooking, estate bottled extra virgin olive for salads and as a condiment, and a small bottle of toasted sesame oil for Asian food. The different oils should be stored in their original glass bottles and kept in a cool, dark place. Keep the lip of each bottle clean, as any oil dribbled down the side or around the top will oxidise and can contaminate the oil in the bottle. It's worth noting that olive oil does not improve with age so use it up.

Rice

Keep a range of different rices on hand, such as a good Italian risotto rice, some basmati rice for Indian recipes, Thai jasmine rice for Asian dishes, and short grain white rice for Japanese food. Store rice in an airtight container in a cool place.

Pasta

Italian dried pasta is usually of much better quality than so-called 'fresh' pasta – a good example of when fresh is not necessarily best. Store dried pasta in an airtight container in a cool place.

Index

aïoli, 62
Alexander's roast chicken on
    potato gratin, 49
asparagus, roasted, panfried steak with
    balsamic vinegar and, 92
avocado, salad of roast chicken and, with
    mustard vinaigrette, *32*, 33

bacon
    mussels with leeks and bacon, 11
    risotto with garden greens
        and bacon, 119
    vegetable and bacon soup
        with pasta, 127
banana semifreddo, 144, *145*
beans, stirfried green, with minced pork
    and egg noodles, 42
beef – *see also* steak
    beef stewed in red wine, 98
    roasted red onion and beef salad, 30
bok choy, panfried fish with stirfried, on
    egg noodles, 143
broccoli, stirfried mushrooms and, with
    spring onion and crab omelette and
    steamed rice, 44, 45

cakes – *see* pound cake
capsicums
    panfried fish with roasted
        capsicum salad, 76, 77
    roasted pumpkin and red
        capsicum soup, 95
carrot, roasted and orange salad, *94*, 95
chicken
    Alexander's roast chicken on
        potato gratin, 49
    basic roast chicken recipe, 48
    chicken drumsticks with red onion,
        potato and rocket sofrito, and pumpkin
        seed vinaigrette, *100*, 101
    roast chicken and avocado salad with
        mustard vinaigrette, *32*, 33
    roast chicken stuffed with herbs and
        Chinese mushrooms, *112*, 113
    roast chicken with lemon and garlic, 48
    roast chicken with pumpkin, couscous
        and herbed yoghurt, 54, *55*
    roast chicken with tomatoes and
        anchovies and herbed spaghetti, 52
    rules for roasting chicken, 48
    spaghetti with roast chicken and
        salsa cruda, 124, *125*
    spiced roast chicken salad, *50*, 51
    stirfried chicken and pineapple with
        glass noodles, 135
    stirfried Provençal vegetables with roast
        chicken and wine vinegar, 43
    sweet soy and ginger chicken with
        stirfried noodles and peanuts, 53
chillies
    chilli omelette with
        spiced potatoes, 20–21
    Chinese egg noodles in chilli ginger
        broth with tofu, 132
    hot spaghetti with parsley, garlic, chilli
        and olive oil, 122
    mussels in chilli broth
        with noodles, 11
    rice noodle salad with stirfried pork and
        chilli omelette, 138

chocolate
    strawberry and dried fruit salad with
        white chocolate semifreddo, 153
    warm chocolate chip pound cake with
        Laurie's raspberry compote and
        clotted cream, 143
chorizo, mussel and fish stew, 102
chutney, fresh mint, 67
coconut pound cake with banana
    semifreddo, 144, *145*
couscous
    Mediterranean vegetable stew with
        spicy couscous, 103
    roast chicken with pumpkin, couscous
        and herbed yoghurt, 54, *55*
coriander and sesame paste, 139
courgette and lemon risotto with
    panfried salmon, 71
crab omelette,
    stirfried mushrooms and broccoli with
        spring onion and, *44*, 45

desserts – *see also* fruit salad; pound cake
    berry trifle with mascarpone, 152
dipping sauce, Vietnamese, *64*, 65
dressing, green Thai, 136

eggplant
    spaghetti with roasted eggplant, lemon,
        anchovies and mint, 126
    teriyaki eye fillet with roasted
        eggplant salad, 63
escabèched snapper salad, 76

fennel, risotto with lemon and, 119
fettuccine – *see* pasta
fish, 157 – *see also* crab; mussels;
        prawns; salmon
    basic recipe, 70
    escabèched snapper salad, 76
    Indian spiced potatoes with panfried fish
        and minted yoghurt, 93
    mussel, fish and chorizo stew, 102
    panfried fish with fresh herbs, glass
        noodles and dipping sauce, *72*, 73
    panfried fish with mussels
        and cream, 14
    panfried fish with parsley and
        caper salad, 34
    panfried fish with roasted
        capsicum salad, 76
    panfried fish with stirfried bok choy on
        egg noodles, 143
    panfried fish with tomato and ginger jam
        and sticky rice, 75
    panfried fish with tomatoes and basil and
        baked potatoes, 74
    panfried snapper with lemon
        and capers, 70
    pumpkin soup with panfried fish and
        coriander oil, *84*, 85
    rules for panfrying, 70
frittata, *22*, 23
fruit salad
    basic recipe, 150
    roasted fruit salad with red wine and
        frozen Muscovado Greek yoghurt, 151
    rules for making, 150
    strawberry and dried fruit salad with
        white chocolate semifreddo, 153

tropical fruit salad with passionfruit
    semifreddo and macadamia
    pound cake, 155

garlic
    roast chicken with lemon and garlic, 48
    stirfried vegetables with garlic
        and ginger, 38
ginger
    Chinese egg noodles in chilli ginger
        broth with tofu, 132
    panfried fish with tomato and ginger jam
        and sticky rice, 75
    stirfried mussels with ginger and
        snow peas, 42
    stirfried vegetables with garlic
        and ginger, 38
    sweet soy and ginger chicken with
        stirfried noodles and peanuts, 53
gremolata, 116

Indian spiced potatoes with panfried fish
    and minted yoghurt, 93

kumara
    kumara, pumpkin and spinach curry
        with coconut rice, 104, *105*
    spice-rubbed lamb short loins with
        roasted kumara and fresh
        mint chutney, 67

lamb
    French lamb and spring vegetable stew
        on 'green' rice, *106*, 107
    lamb shank stew with pumpkin risotto
        and gremolata, 116, *117*
    spice-rubbed lamb short loins with roasted
        kumara and fresh mint chutney, 67
leeks and bacon, mussels with, 11
lemons
    lemon and courgette risotto with
        panfried salmon, 71
    lemon mayonnaise, 13
    lemon syrup pound cake with
        roasted peaches, *146* 147
    risotto with lemon and fennel, 119
    roast chicken with lemon and garlic, 48
    roasted field mushrooms with lemon and
        tarragon cream on fettuccine, 124
    spaghetti with roasted eggplant, lemon,
        anchovies and mint, 126

macadamia pound cake, 155
mayonnaise
    aïoli, 62
    lemon mayonnaise, 13
mushrooms
    roast chicken stuffed with herbs and
        Chinese mushrooms, *112*, 113
    roasted field mushrooms with lemon and
        tarragon cream on fettuccine, 124
    stirfried mushrooms and broccoli with
        spring onion and crab omelette and
        steamed rice, *44*, 45
mussels
    basic recipe, 10
    creamed mussel and spinach soup, 81
    mussel, fish and chorizo stew, 102
    mussel, spinach and potato salad, 30, *31*
    mussels in chilli broth with noodles, 11

mussels with herbed rice and lemon
    mayonnaise, *12*, 13
mussels with leeks and bacon, 11
panfried fish with mussels and cream, 14
rules for cleaning and cooking, 10
steamed mussels on noodles with
    coriander and sesame paste, 139
steamed mussels with white wine, 10
stirfried Chinese greens with mussels, 14, *15*
stirfried mussels with ginger and
    snow peas, 42
tomato sofrito and mussels
    with pasta, 102
warm mussel and rice salad, 114
mustard vinaigrette, 33

noodles
    basic recipe, 132
    Chinese egg noodles in chilli ginger
        broth with tofu, 132
    mussels in chilli broth with noodles, 11
    panfried fish with fresh herbs, glass
        noodles and dipping sauce, *72*, 73
    panfried fish with stirfried bok choy on
        egg noodles, 143
    prawn omelette with cold rice
        noodle salad, 24, *25*
    rice noodle salad with stirfried pork and
        chilli omelette, 138
    rules for cooking, 133
    sliced steak on egg noodles with green
        Thai dressing, 136, *137*
    steamed mussels on noodles with
        coriander and sesame paste, 139
    stirfried chicken and pineapple with
        glass noodles, 135
    stirfried green beans with minced pork
        and egg noodles, 42
    sweet soy and ginger chicken with
        stirfried noodles and peanuts, 53

olive, rocket, tomato and bread salad,
    panfried steak on, 35
omelettes
    basic recipe, 18
    chilli omelette with
        spiced potatoes, 20–21
    fresh herb omelette, 18
    prawn omelette with cold rice
        noodle salad, 24, *25*
    rice noodle salad with stirfried pork and
        chilli omelette, 138
    roasted pumpkin and feta frittata, 22, 23
    rules for making, 19
    spicy pork omelette with fried rice, 21
    stirfried mushrooms and broccoli with
        spring onion and crab omelette and
        steamed rice, 44, 45
    tortilla de patatas, 20
onions
    chicken drumsticks with red onion,
        potato and rocket sofrito, and pumpkin
        seed vinaigrette, *100*, 101
    panfried sirloin steak with
        red onions, *60*, 61
    roasted red onion and beef salad, 30
    roasted red onion and potato soup with
        parmesan croutons, 82
    steamed shellfish with potatoes and
        onions on spaghetti, 127
oranges
    orange and polenta pound cake with
        prune and port semifreddo, 147
    roasted carrot and orange salad, *94*, 95

passionfruit semifreddo, 155
pasta
    basic recipe, 122
    chunky Italian-style vegetable soup with
        tubular pasta, 83
    hot spaghetti with parsley, garlic, chilli
        and olive oil, 122
    hot spaghetti with tomatoes, rocket,
        parmesan and balsamic vinegar, 34
    roast chicken with tomatoes and
        anchovies and herbed spaghetti, 52
    roasted field mushrooms with lemon and
        tarragon cream on fettuccine, 124
    rules for cooking, 123
    spaghetti with roast chicken and
        salsa cruda, 124, *125*
    spaghetti with roasted eggplant, lemon,
        anchovies and mint, 126
    steamed shellfish with potatoes and
        onions on spaghetti, 127
    tomato sofrito and mussels with pasta, 102
    vegetable and bacon soup with pasta, 127
    warm penne and roasted
        vegetable salad, *128*, 129
peaches, roasted, lemon syrup pound
    cake with, *146*, 147
peas, stirfried mussels with ginger and
    snow peas, 42
pilaf, pumpkin and almond,
    with harissa, 115
pineapple, stirfried chicken and, with
    glass noodles, 135
polenta, and orange pound cake, with
    prune and port semifreddo, 147
pork – see also bacon
    rice noodle salad with stirfried pork and
        chilli omelette, 138
    spicy pork omelette with fried rice, 21
    stirfried green beans with minced pork
        and egg noodles, 42
potatoes
    Alexander's roast chicken on
        potato gratin, 49
    chicken drumsticks with red onion,
        potato and rocket sofrito, and pumpkin
        seed vinaigrette, *100*, 101
    chilli omelette with spiced potatoes, 20–21
    Indian spiced potatoes with panfried fish
        and minted yoghurt, 93
    mussel, spinach and potato salad, 30, *31*
    panfried fish with tomatoes and basil and
        baked potatoes, 74
    panfried rump steak with potato and
        rocket stew, 66
    roasted red onion and potato soup with
        parmesan croûtons, 82
    steamed shellfish with potatoes and
        onions on spaghetti, 127
    tortilla de patatas, 20
pound cake
    basic recipe, 142
    coconut pound cake with
        banana semifreddo, 144, *145*
    lemon syrup pound cake with
        roasted peaches, *146* 147
    orange and polenta pound cake with
        prune and port semifreddo, 147
    rules for making, 142
    summer pound cake pudding, 152
    toasted pound cake with fresh berries
        and Greek yoghurt, 143
    tropical fruit salad with passionfruit
        semifreddo and macadamia
        pound cake, 155

warm chocolate chip pound cake with
    Laurie's raspberry compote and
    clotted cream, 143
prawn omelette with cold rice
    noodle salad, 24, *25*
prune and port semifreddo, 147
pumpkin
    kumara, pumpkin and spinach curry with
        coconut rice, 104, *105*
    lamb shank stew with pumpkin risotto
        and gremolata, 116, *117*
    pumpkin and almond pilaf
        with harissa, 115
    pumpkin soup with panfried fish and
        coriander oil, *84*, 85
    roast chicken with pumpkin, couscous
        and herbed yoghurt, 54, *55*
    roasted pumpkin and feta frittata, *22*, 23
    roasted pumpkin and red
        capsicum soup, 95

raspberry compote, Laurie's, warm
    chocolate chip pound cake and clotted
    cream with, 143
rice, 157 – see also risotto
    curry spiced tomato and rice soup, 81
    French lamb and spring vegetable stew
        on 'green' rice, *106*, 107
    kumara, pumpkin and spinach curry with
        coconut rice, 104, *105*
    mussels with herbed rice and
        lemon mayonnaise, *12*,13
    panfried fish with tomato and ginger jam
        and sticky rice, 75
    prawn omelette with cold rice
        noodle salad, 24, *25*
    pumpkin and almond pilaf
        with harissa, 115
    rice noodle salad with stirfried pork and
        chilli omelette, 138
    roast chicken stuffed with herbs and
        Chinese mushrooms, *112*, 113
    rules for cooking, 111
    sliced steak with vegetable
        fried rice, 40, *41*
    spicy pork omelette with fried rice, 21
    steamed white rice, 110
    stirfried mushrooms and broccoli with
        spring onion and crab omelette and
        steamed rice, *44*, 45
    warm mussel and rice salad, 114
risotto
    basic recipe, 110
    fresh herb risotto, 110
    lamb shank stew with pumpkin risotto
        and gremolata, 116, *117*
    lemon and courgette risotto with
        panfried salmon, 71
    parmesan risotto with roasted
        vegetables, 118
    risotto with garden greens
        and bacon, 119
    risotto with lemon and fennel, 119
    rules for making, 111
roast chicken – see chicken

rocket
    chicken drumsticks with red onion,
        potato and rocket sofrito, and pumpkin
        seed vinaigrette, *100*, 101
    hot spaghetti with tomatoes, rocket,
        parmesan and balsamic vinegar, 34
    panfried rump steak with potato and
        rocket stew, 66

panfried salmon with warm roasted
tomato vinaigrette and rocket, 90, *91*
panfried steak on olive, rocket, tomato
and bread salad, 35

salad
basic recipe, 28
escabèched snapper salad, 76
green salad with vinaigrette, 28
hot spaghetti with tomatoes, rocket,
parmesan and balsamic vinegar, 34
mussel, spinach and potato salad, 30, *31*
panfried fish with parsley and
caper salad, 34
panfried fish with roasted
capsicum salad, 76, *77*
panfried steak on olive, rocket, tomato
and bread salad, 35
prawn omelette with cold rice
noodle salad, 24, *25*
rice noodle salad with stirfried pork and
chilli omelette, 138
roast chicken and avocado salad with
mustard vinaigrette, *32, 33*
roasted carrot and orange salad, *94, 95*
roasted red onion and beef salad, 30
spiced roast chicken salad, 50, *51*
rules for making, 29
teriyaki eye fillet with roasted
eggplant salad, 63
warm mussel and rice salad, 114
warm penne and roasted
vegetable salad, *128, 129*
salmon
lemon and courgette risotto with
panfried salmon, 71
panfried salmon with warm roasted
tomato vinaigrette and rocket, 90, *91*
salsa cruda, 124
semifreddo
banana, 144, *145*
passionfruit, 155
prune and port, 147
rules for making, 144
white chocolate, 153
snow peas, stirfried mussels with
ginger and, 42
sofrito
red onion, potato and rocket, 101
tomato, 102
soup
basic recipe, 80
chunky Italian-style vegetable soup
with tubular pasta, 83
curry spiced tomato and rice soup, 81
'French' vegetable soup, 80
pumpkin soup with panfried fish and
coriander oil, *84, 85*
roasted pumpkin and red
capsicum soup, 95
roasted red onion and potato soup
with parmesan croûtons, 82
rules for making, 80
vegetable and bacon soup
with pasta, 127
spaghetti – see pasta

spinach
creamed mussel and spinach soup, 81
kumara, pumpkin and spinach curry
with coconut rice, 104
mussel, spinach and potato salad, 30, *31*
steak
basic recipe, 50
minute steak sandwich with roasted
vegetables and aïoli, 62
panfried eye fillet with pan juices and
wholegrain mustard, 50
panfried rump steak with potato and
rocket stew, 66
panfried sirloin steak with
red onions, *60*, 61
panfried steak on olive, rocket, tomato
and bread salad, 35
panfried steak with balsamic vinegar and
roasted asparagus, 92
rules for cooking, 59
sliced steak on egg noodles with green
Thai dressing, 136, *137*
sliced steak with vegetable
fried rice, 40, *41*
spice-rubbed lamb short loins with
roasted kumara and fresh
mint chutney, 67
teriyaki eye fillet with roasted
eggplant salad, 63
Vietnamese-style steak with rice,
vegetables and dipping sauce, 64, *65*
stew
basic recipe, 98
beef stewed in red wine, 98
chicken drumsticks with red onion,
potato and rocket sofrito, and pumpkin
seed vinaigrette, *100, 101*
French lamb and spring vegetable stew
on 'green' rice, *106, 107*
kumara, pumpkin and spinach curry with
coconut rice, 104, *105*
lamb shank stew with pumpkin risotto
and gremolata, 116, *117*
Mediterranean vegetable stew with
spicy couscous, 103
mussel, fish and chorizo stew, 102
rules for stew, 99
tomato sofrito and mussels with pasta, 102
stirfries
basic recipe, 38
rice noodle salad with stirfried pork and
chilli omelette, 138
rules for stirfrying, 39
sliced steak with vegetable
fried rice, 40, *41*
stirfried Chinese greens
with mussels, 14, *15*
stirfried green beans with minced pork
and egg noodles, 42
stirfried mushrooms and broccoli with
spring onion and crab omelette and
steamed rice, *44, 45*
stirfried mussels with ginger and
snow peas, 42
stirfried Provençal vegetables with roast
chicken and wine vinegar, 43
stirfried vegetables with garlic
and ginger, 38

sweet soy and ginger chicken with
stirfried noodles and peanuts, 53
strawberry and dried fruit salad with white
chocolate semifreddo, 153

teriyaki eye fillet with roasted
eggplant salad, 63
tofu, Chinese egg noodles in chilli ginger
broth with, 132
trifle, berry, with mascarpone, 152
tomatoes
curry spiced tomato and rice soup, 81
hot spaghetti with tomatoes, rocket,
parmesan and balsamic vinegar, 34
panfried fish with tomato and ginger jam
and sticky rice, 75
panfried fish with tomatoes and basil and
baked potatoes, 74
panfried salmon with warm roasted
tomato vinaigrette and rocket, 90, *91*
panfried steak on olive, rocket, tomato
and bread salad, 35
roast chicken with tomatoes and
anchovies and herbed spaghetti, 52
tortilla de patatas, 20

vegetables – *see also* specific vegetables,
for example, potatoes
French lamb and spring vegetable stew
on 'green' rice, *106, 107*
Mediterranean vegetable stew with
spicy couscous, 103
minute steak sandwich with roasted
vegetables and aïoli, 62
parmesan risotto with
roasted vegetables, 118
risotto with garden greens
and bacon, 119
sliced steak with vegetable
fried rice, 40, *41*
stirfried Chinese greens
with mussels, 14, *15*
stirfried Provençal vegetables with roast
chicken and wine vinegar, 43
stirfried vegetables with garlic
and ginger, 38
vegetable and bacon soup with pasta, 127
warm penne and roasted vegetable
salad, *128, 129*
Vietnamese-style steak with rice,
vegetables and dipping sauce, 64, *65*
vinaigrette, 28
basil, 35
mustard, 33
pumpkin seed, 101
warm roasted tomato, 90

yoghurt
Indian spiced potatoes with panfried fish
and minted yoghurt, 93
roast chicken with pumpkin, couscous
and herbed yoghurt, 54, *55*
roasted fruit salad with red wine and
frozen Muscovado Greek yoghurt, 151
toasted pound cake with fresh berries
and Greek yoghurt, 143

Grateful thanks to The Studio of Tableware, Auckland,
for their help with props.